# MIDTOWN CAFE 35TH ANNIVERSARY
## STORIES · PEOPLE · RECIPES

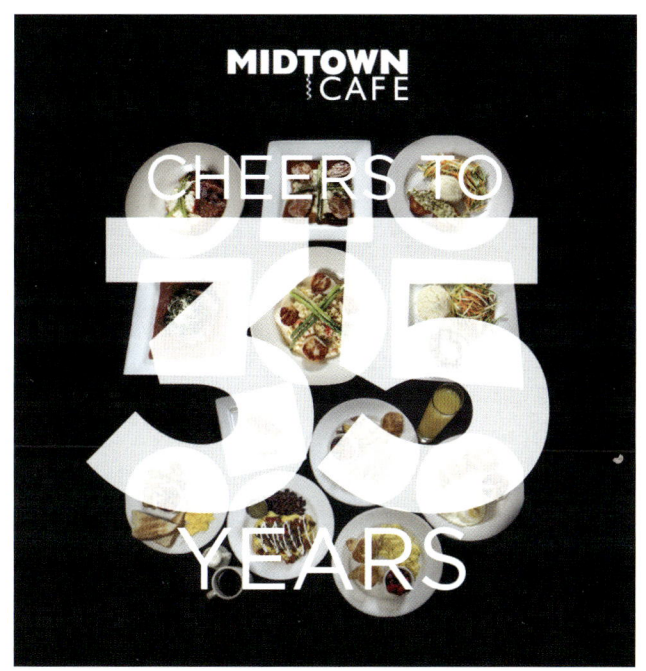

**MIDTOWN CAFE**

CHEERS TO
35
YEARS

## KARREN PELL AND RANDY RAYBURN

ISBN 979-8-218-03920-2

Printed in USA

Art on cover of Midtown Cafe and Sunset Grill Copyright ©Sam Dunlap
Book design: Christa Schoenbrodt, Studio Haus
Midtown Anniversary logo: Chris Climer

www.MidtownCafe.com

# TABLE OF CONTENTS

DEDICATIONS . . . . . . . . . . . . . . . . . . . . . . . . . . . . . . . . . . . . vii

ACKNOWLEDGMENTS. . . . . . . . . . . . . . . . . . . . . . . . . . . . . . . ix

AUTHOR'S NOTE (RANDY). . . . . . . . . . . . . . . . . . . . . . . . . .x

HAPPY ANNIVERSARY (RANDY & KARREN) . . . . . . . . . . xi

A LITTLE BIT OF HISTORY (KARREN). . . . . . . . . . . . . . . . . .1

## MIDTOWN CAFE STORIES

Origin of Midtown . . . . . . . . . . . . . . . . . . . . . . . . . . . . . . 4

How the Kitchen Goes . . . . . . . . . . . . . . . . . . . . . . . . . 8

## MIDTOWN CAFE PEOPLE

Chef Brian Uhl . . . . . . . . . . . . . . . . . . . . . . . . . . . . . . . 11

Dale King. . . . . . . . . . . . . . . . . . . . . . . . . . . . . . . . . . . .13

Doug Stevenson. . . . . . . . . . . . . . . . . . . . . . . . . . . . . .16

Gemma Freidli . . . . . . . . . . . . . . . . . . . . . . . . . . . . . . .19

Gina Kochevar . . . . . . . . . . . . . . . . . . . . . . . . . . . . . . .21

Jerry Baxter . . . . . . . . . . . . . . . . . . . . . . . . . . . . . . . . . 23

John Woodard . . . . . . . . . . . . . . . . . . . . . . . . . . . . . . . 27

Chef Max Pastor. . . . . . . . . . . . . . . . . . . . . . . . . . . . . 29

Miguel Martinez . . . . . . . . . . . . . . . . . . . . . . . . . . . . . .31

## SUNSET GRILL STORIES

Opening Up Sunset Grill. . . . . . . . . . . . . . . . . . . . . . . 32

The Patio. . . . . . . . . . . . . . . . . . . . . . . . . . . . . . . . . . . 36

Saying Good-Bye To Sunset. . . . . . . . . . . . . . . . . . . . 38

## SUNSET GRILL PEOPLE

Chris Climer . . . . . . . . . . . . . . . . . . . . . . . . . . . . . . . . 39

Craig Clifft. . . . . . . . . . . . . . . . . . . . . . . . . . . . . . . . . .41

Dano Goosetree. . . . . . . . . . . . . . . . . . . . . . . . . . . . . 43

Dese Hayes. . . . . . . . . . . . . . . . . . . . . . . . . . . . . . . . . 45

Lynda Herdelin. . . . . . . . . . . . . . . . . . . . . . . . . . . . . . 47

Manuel Zeitlin. . . . . . . . . . . . . . . . . . . . . . . . . . . . . . . 49

Marilyn Merdler . . . . . . . . . . . . . . . . . . . . . . . . . . . . . 52

Michael Hunt. . . . . . . . . . . . . . . . . . . . . . . . . . . . . . . .54

Paul Harmon. . . . . . . . . . . . . . . . . . . . . . . . . . . . . . . . . . . . . . . 56
Pompie Horner. . . . . . . . . . . . . . . . . . . . . . . . . . . . . . . . . . . . . 59
Rick Sanjek . . . . . . . . . . . . . . . . . . . . . . . . . . . . . . . . . . . . . . . .61
Robynne Napier . . . . . . . . . . . . . . . . . . . . . . . . . . . . . . . . . . . . 64
Suzanne Coleman . . . . . . . . . . . . . . . . . . . . . . . . . . . . . . . . . . 67

RANDY RAYBURN . . . . . . . . . . . . . . . . . . . . . . . . . . . . . . . . 70
NEVER GIVE UP . . . . . . . . . . . . . . . . . . . . . . . . . . . . . . . . . . 75

RECIPES
Breakfast
Fried Green Tomatoes Benedict . . . . . . . . . . . . . . . . . . . . . . 79
Nashville Pigs In A Blanket . . . . . . . . . . . . . . . . . . . . . . . . . .81
Chef Brian's French Toast . . . . . . . . . . . . . . . . . . . . . . . . . . 83
Appetizers
Chicken Croquettes. . . . . . . . . . . . . . . . . . . . . . . . . . . . . . . . 84
Crispy Brussels Sprouts . . . . . . . . . . . . . . . . . . . . . . . . . . . . 86
Lemon Artichoke Soup. . . . . . . . . . . . . . . . . . . . . . . . . . . . . 87
Entrees
Caesar Salad With Salmon. . . . . . . . . . . . . . . . . . . . . . . . . . 88
Mediterranean Pasta. . . . . . . . . . . . . . . . . . . . . . . . . . . . . . . 89
Voodoo Pasta . . . . . . . . . . . . . . . . . . . . . . . . . . . . . . . . . . . . 90
Shrimp And Grits. . . . . . . . . . . . . . . . . . . . . . . . . . . . . . . . .91
Midtown Meatloaf . . . . . . . . . . . . . . . . . . . . . . . . . . . . . . . . 92
Chicken Puff Pastry. . . . . . . . . . . . . . . . . . . . . . . . . . . . . . . 94
Rainbow Trout . . . . . . . . . . . . . . . . . . . . . . . . . . . . . . . . . . . 95
Desserts
Habanero Butterscotch Bread Pudding . . . . . . . . . . . . . . . . 96
Jack Daniel's Chocolate Pecan Pie . . . . . . . . . . . . . . . . . . . 97
Creme Brulee . . . . . . . . . . . . . . . . . . . . . . . . . . . . . . . . . . . . 98

SELECTED BIBLIOGRAPHY. . . . . . . . . . . . . . . . . . . . . . . . 99
ABOUT THE AUTHORS. . . . . . . . . . . . . . . . . . . . . . . . . . . 100

# WHAT THEY'RE SAYING ABOUT MIDTOWN AND DA MAN!

Rated one of the TOP 50 Best Southern Restaurants in America According to Open Table-Food and Wine Magazine

*"Midtown Cafe offers the best in affordable, casual fine dining. A little jewel."*
— American Cuisine.com, The Culinary Encyclopedia of America

*"In his illustrious career, Randy Rayburn has built a reputation that is not just unrivaled in the hospitality industry but reaches deeply and generously into Nashville's many communities—arts, entertainment, sports, business, politics and philanthropy. There is not a decade on Nashville's timeline of the last 50 years where his name is not included, and his influence not felt. Few in the business have more stories, or more trust when it comes to keeping confidences. I have often said that Randy Rayburn has hired, fired, or fed most everyone who has lived, or passed through Nashville, and has remained friends with most of them. There is simply no one like him."*
— Kay West

*"Charming long-time Music Row destination Midtown Cafe is a Nashville staple from Randy Rayburn. Open for over 30 years, the cozy little cafe known for its lemon arti- choke soup transports diners back to the Nashville before the influx of bro-country and bachelorettes."*
— Delia Jo Ramsey, Eater.com, Feb 7, 2022

Listed as "One of 20 Great Spots for a Monday Meal Out" (Feb 7 2020) & "21 Excellent Date Night Restaurants in Nashville (Sept 8 2021)," Delia Jo Ramsey. Eater.com

# DEDICATIONS

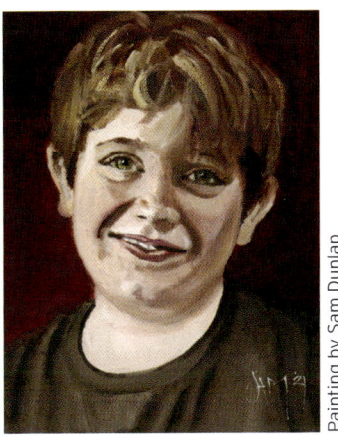
Painting by Sam Dunlap

Painting by Sam Dunlap

## FROM RANDY

*For my part, I dedicate this book to my sons, Duke Rainier Rayburn and Dean Emmett Rayburn, who give me inspiration and the joy in life so that I can rise and embrace every day.*

## FROM KARREN

*For my part, I dedicate this book to my friends from the old days at Sunset Grill and to my friends from the now days at Midtown Cafe. You are all a blessing in my life, and I love and appreciate you.*

# ACKNOWLEDGMENTS

In its own way, a book is a living being. And like any living being, it is brought to physical reality through the effort of and giving from other beings. Love is not always involved, but in the case of this book, on at least one level of creation, it was a labor of love. So now that the book is here among us, some acknowledgment of those who made it real is appropriate, and Randy and I are honored and grateful to do so.

## FROM KARREN

First, I thank my co-conspirator and life brother Randy Rayburn without whose gifts of manifestation this work would not be a book. I also thank him for being my friend and making room for me in his life for all these decades—my life is better for him being in it. And then there is the fact that he saved my ass more than once, and therefore I was around to write this book. And speaking of being around, I am in debt to my long-suffering husband, Tim Henderson, who has endured a year of a wife who disappeared every day into her office, who caused all house renovations to be put on hold. Thank you, Tim. I do love my hubby. I much appreciate my bestie, Carole King (and co-writer of 4 books) for her help. Kudos to my bud and neighbor, Cindy Clark, for creating the mock-ups that got our creative juices flowing. To my Sunset and Midtown friends, thank you for your help on this book and for the light you shine in my life. To Mary Skinner, my long-time dear friend, my thanks for referring me to Twyla Lambert Clark. And to Twyla Lambert Clark, please accept my gratitude for the expertise, knowledge, patience, and transformational energy it took to bring the book from my desk to the press. And I much appreciate Twyla for referring me to graphic artist Christa Schoenbrodt whose connection, artistry, and patience took this book to a higher level and played a role in its manifestation. It took a village. I could go on and on. Hell, I'm thankful for the sunlight that blessed my desk with natural light and the old window it shined through, and for anyone who has read this far: thank you.

## FROM RANDY

Karren covered most of the village we are thankful for. I want to add many thanks and blessings to the fantastic work families, our friends, and our guests of Midtown Cafe. Thanks goes to Sam Dunlap for the amazing portraits of my sons and of Sunset Grill and Midtown Cafe. Chris Climer also gets kudos for help locating images and helping us get them to Christa. Additionally, appreciation and blessings to Karren Pell, author, singer, songwriter, troubadour, and my adopted in life sister, for putting up with me for almost four decades and for all it took to finally bring this evolved vision to print. It does take a village, and I am grateful for every single member.

# SPECIAL THANKS

Painting by Sam Dunlap

## FROM RANDY

I feel the need to thank certain people in writing for helping my survival and relative success in life up to this point. This book is a summation of a celebration of life for all the wonderful people in my life along the way.

So I am thankful for my working families and the literally millions of guests that have passed through and blessed my almost five decades of restaurant life chapters opening Sunset Grill, Cabana, Moonbeams, The Marc, F. Scott's, Third Coast, Mere Bulles, Dunham Station, Tavern on the Row, Rhett's & Jack Daniel's Saloon-Gaylord Opryland Hotel, and Café Ritz and others.

I want to especially thank my dearest friend and investor in Sunset Grill, Rick Sanjek, for believing in me and giving me my first real restaurant job bussing tables in 1975 while I was going to law school. Kudos and respect to Cabana operating partners Craig Clifft and Chef Brian Uhl. Also Gary Smith and Rob Taylor, CPAs; attorneys Irwin Venick, John Nelley, Larry Stewart, and Tom White for helping guide the business process. Additional love to my friend and mentor Jerry "Julian" Baxter; Craig Clifft, my business partner and friend; and my PastaBrothers in life David Bennett, Ray Harris, Don Roy, Chef Paul Brennan, Raymond Thomason, Bill Bomar, Omari Booker, Mickey Despot, and Grady Utley.

And offering my eternal love to my mother, Kathleen, my grandmother, Georgia Butler, and my father, Guy Rayburn, for their love in raising me in Milan, Tennessee on a twenty-seven-acre farm.

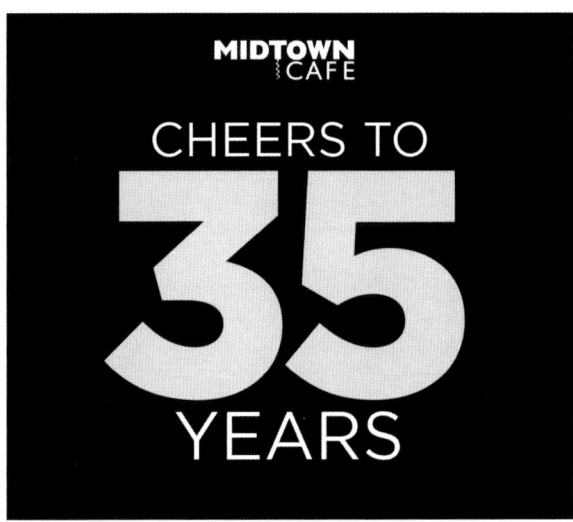

## FROM RANDY

'm a Lord of the Rings fan since my college days. I have probably read that series 8, 10, 12 times; I've lost track. I thought the later set of movies were quite excellent. So since the time I started my own journey by selling my home and opening the Sunset Grill, I have named all my companies for characters from Lord of the Rings. There was Gandalf and Bilbo and Frodo and Aragorn and Eowyn; you know, it was one of those things. When we took over Midtown Cafe on September 2, 1997, I named it Gandalf, LLC. My banker thought it was pretty weird, but other than that it was wonderful. And so here, on our 35th Anniversary, I thought a quote from Gandalf would be appropriate: "All we have to decide is what to do with the time that is given to us."

So we decided to stand together. And stand we have. We've stood through loss, change, fear, and even flood, tornado, and pestilence. Now, in observing our 35th anniversary, we stand at this point where we are able to celebrate.

I'll just say that I'm blessed to have the great management team of Midtown Cafe with both Doug Stevenson of 27 years and Gina Kochevar of 21 years, along with Gemma Freidli of 11 years, and John Woodard in the front of the house who returned from 20 years ago. For over 30 years I've been honored to have Craig Clifft as a protégé. Any coach is only as good as his team's players. In the back of the house, I'm thankful to cruise along with Chef Max Pastor and Sous Chef Miguel Martinez and other longtime employees in front and back of the house. Any coach is only as good as his team. He surrounds himself with team members that get along and work well together and the customers know it. The key to Midtown Cafe is that the team enjoys serving the public. I was born to serve. It took me a long time to figure that out. As Bob Dylan said so eloquently, "You gotta serve somebody." I figured it out a long time ago, and I still enjoy doing it and will do it as long as I can—until I am no longer able.

So we stand here where the friends, the guests, the promoters, the artists, the designers, the investors, the culinary staff, the serving staff are together and can drink a toast to each other.

I stand here to thank my working family—Midtown Cafe—for so much loving and caring. I love you too.

We decided to stand, and I'm glad we did. Happy Anniversary.

Excelsior,
Randy Rayburn


## FROM KARREN

When the Sunset Grill closed, I was truly broken hearted. It had been my home base for the many years of what I now refer to as my gypsy period. When I finally put down roots in Alabama, I still considered the Sunset Grill my home away from home and Randy and the staff my Nashville family. But I continued to regularly visit my friends in Nashville and during that time I'd meet with Randy, Jerry and Suzanne at Midtown Cafe. I have always loved the feel of it. I have always been happy to see familiar faces like Dale, Doug, and John. I came to look forward to seeing Gina, and besides she fixes a mean Mimosa. So it was that Midtown Cafe took the place of Sunset Grill in my heart.

It's been a scary wild ride these past few years. I kept in touch, and hubby Tim and I helped when we could. I continued to hope and pray that everyone at Midtown came through okay and for the most part, they did. I'm proud and happy for them.

I hope this book shows my affection for them and my appreciation of their work.

Like Randy, I am a Tolkien fan. My fellow wanderer, Bilbo Baggins, said this and it seems to fit: "The road goes ever on and on." I am thankful for the part of the road I traveled that led to Midtown.

Happy Anniversary,
Karren Pell

# A LITTLE BIT OF HISTORY

While Randy Rayburn, owner and proprietor of the Sunset Grill, had worked at several famous restaurants in Nashville before opening the Sunset Grill, what could be called the "Sunset Seed" started to seriously germinate at "The Tavern on the Row" after he returned from the Culinary Institute of America in Hyde Park, New York. The "row" refers to none other than "Music Row"- two one-way streets, 16th and 17th Avenue -as in "God bless the boys who make the noise on 16th Avenue." Much has changed on those one-way streets since I lugged my guitar and cassette tapes around (anybody remember them). In my time, the early 1900 historic homes had been converted into mostly music publisher offices, studios, and management businesses. I and other writers could walk to writing appointments (most songs were co-written) and "pitch appointments," (meetings with record executives to play my songs-hoping they would keep one to play for their producers). Shady trees along sidewalks, shortcuts down the alleys and between buildings, and homey offices in the parlors of those old houses created a kind of "campus" vibe but make no mistake—the music biz organizations housed on those two streets could make or break the dreams of singers and songwriters like me in a "9-5" fashion. The "Tavern" was a 1920s home (as was all of Music Row at one time) turned restaurant/bar in the late 1980s. After a hard day's work writing songs, listening to songs, reading contracts (surely some of them read the contracts) and signing contracts (some of them signed contracts), making those all-important-connections, and well, business as usual, music biz types gathered at the Tavern on the Row, their favorite watering hole. In the evenings, singers, songwriters, and their entourages, continued the revelry. Wayland, Willie, and the boys were recording next door; "Island," a hot LA based rock 'n' roll publishing company, had opened an office across the street; the Tavern's brick courtyard allowed everyone to see and be seen. The Tavern on the Row was the place to be.

So, like the song said, "there we all were in one place." Or at least quite a few of us. Randy Rayburn and Bill Sims were managers, Dano Goosetree ran the bar, and yours truly worked as a bookkeeper. I had received no specific training from the previous bookkeeper as, I was told, "one day she just disappeared." I confess to being a tad naïve at that time, having come from rural North Carolina to chase my dream of being a songwriter. Yep, just like you read about, I had left a tenured teaching position, sold a three-bedroom brick house and most of what was in it, packed my guitar and demo tapes and whatever else fit into my Ford Escort station wagon, and drove across the Blue Ridge Mountains to Nashville, Tennessee. I rented a small apartment in an old house on Belmont Boulevard, and after working all day, I went out at night listening to famous songwriters render their hit songs at the Blue Bird Cafe, dreaming one day that would be me. Dreaming. There was a lot of dreaming going on.

*Karren Pell and Randy Rayburn celebrating at Circa.*

But it wasn't all dreaming as I developed a case of the nerves about that bookkeeping job and decided maybe I needed to "just disappear" from that job too. As I said, while I was naive, I was not completely oblivious to the fact that I was a single woman, alone with no friends in a big city. What to do? What to do?

I had not really made any friends yet. I was obsessed with the music biz. I caught on early that the players functioned in a rather maze-like business structure, and the key to finding the way to a big hit jackpot was social relationships. I was working on figuring out how I could get in the club. My immediate goal was to have some days off to write songs and hang out at publishing houses that encouraged new writers. So, making new buddies had not been a priority. While I needed a job to pay rent on that little apartment, I also needed to do something about my case of the nerves. Suddenly, I needed a friend.

The manager, Randy Rayburn, looked like a straight shooter to me. He and the owner fought often. I decided to take a chance (now that I look back, along with the dreaming there was a lot of chance taking). As I described, the restaurant was in a house dated around 1920. My office was upstairs. There were some tables on the second floor, but most of the restaurant was on the first floor and on the large patio in the front of the building. One day, I saw Randy working downstairs, and no one else was around. I went to him and told him about my case of the nerves. He stood up from bending over a table he was cleaning and looked me in the eye. Sizing me up, I guess. Then he also took a chance. He said he also had a case of the nerves. He said we were getting out of there. I liked the plural pronoun. He said he was opening the Third Coast. Did I want to be the hostess? What the hell-why not? He said not to give the Tavern a notice. He said wait a few days and he would send for me. Sure enough—in a few days he left. A few days later Dano, the bartender, left. Just as my case of the nerves was spiking, I received a handwritten note delivered by a young man I did not know. It said "Now." I got up from my desk and left the Tavern on the Row. From there I walked the three blocks over to the Third Coast. When I opened the front door, Randy and Dano waved hello. Now I had friends.

Later Tavern on the Row closed. But my friends and I were at the Third Coast. And that's how it all started. (Karren Pell)

*Randy Rayburn with artist Paul Harmon's* Walking Man *at Midtown Cafe*

# MIDTOWN CAFE STORIES

used to enjoy dining in Midtown Cafe occasionally on Sunday nights when Sunset Grill was closed, and it's one of those strange mysteries of life that, I loved it so much, I bought it. I'd added another dining room to the Sunset Grill and then added a retractable roof on the patio (don't ever do that retractable thing; that was a big leaking mistake). But anyway, I wound up looking for other options for expanding and diversifying because I didn't want all my eggs in one basket at Sunset Grill. So, I looked at other restaurant locations to open or take over.

John Petrocelli, the owner of Midtown Cafe, had opened Midtown Cafe in 1987 with Curt Cole, who later moved to Washington D. C. One day John called me up looking for a night manager.

"What's going on, John?" I asked.

"Well," John replied, "I'm wanting to sell, but I need someone to manage it in the meantime 'cause I'm tired of working nights, and my wife is tired of me working nights, and I really want to stay married."

I responded, "Well John, I told you a long time ago that if you ever wanted to sell Midtown Cafe, that I liked it a lot, and we should talk. So let's talk."

So, we did talk, and I realized there was an opportunity there. Midtown was a small, intimate restaurant that was very different from Sunset Grill, but very similar in that it was small and upscale with good quality food. I visited one or two times a month on Sunday nights to relax and sit in what was then the bar area. I enjoyed bantering with

*Midtown Old Timers Patrick Petzcko, Mike Wyatt, Doug Stevenson, Gina Kochevar & Dale King.*

*Left: 2022's management team.*

*Midtown has been tucked in between Broadway and West End on 19th Avenue in Nashville, Tennessee for over 35 years.*

the staff and had a nice simple meal, a Caesar salad and something, and went on home to get an early night's rest for the week ahead. I needed to stay working at Sunset, and since I couldn't be two places at once, I knew that my best friend, Jerry Baxter, who was managing Sunset, was very capable of running the restaurant. Jerry is my lifelong best friend and former roommate from times past at Squirrel Hill. Jerry had opened the Brass Scales in 1971, and later Julian's in 1974, and then came back and opened Sperry's in 1975. He then managed a number of other restaurants for other people, although he'd been 25% owner of the Brass Scales and the court eventually awarded him 50% ownership of Julian's. I also had some other additional team members whom I thought would transition well from Sunset to Midtown.

So I talked with John Nelley (my wine/traveling friend, CPA, and lawyer) and acquiring Midtown Cafe seemed to be a really good idea. John Petrocelli was wanting a reasonable multiple over EBITDA (earnings before interest, taxes, depreciation, and amortization) paid out over five years. It seemed to be a good business; it was making a little bit over a million dollars a year in 1997, which for an 80-seat restaurant including six barstools, was a pretty good situation. The dining room held about seventeen tables, and there were a couple of tables in the bar area, so it was really a nice, small, intimate restaurant about the size of Sunset Grill's main dining room, or as many tables on the inside as Sunset Grill's patio. As part of the deal, we got the recipe for the lemon artichoke soup. John Nelley came in as 5% investor-business partner. We took Midtown Cafe over September 2, 1997.

Craig Clifft led the charge on technology and working with Jerry, and I worked on improving the menu. I didn't want Craig to move over there because I needed him at Sunset Grill as general manager because it was a bigger, more successful restaurant-day and night six days a week. With the addition of the Sunset dining room, we were doing around five or six million dollars a year in annual sales at Sunset. Midtown was quaint; it catered to a little bit of an older West Nashville crowd and was really a nice little shining star.

Midtown was a wonderful place that I realized that I would try to put my stamp on. It was not my intent to be there every day because I was at Sunset. I wanted it to have its own flavor and style totally different from Sunset. Midtown was something that I would go and spend maybe one meeting a week with management, both front and back of the house. We'd talk about things that needed to be done, but I didn't have to spend a whole lot of time there. I tried to eat there maybe once or twice a week in order to keep up with the quality of the food and to experience what the customers were experiencing without trying to be a hands-on management. I think that Midtown satisfied my need for another quality, white tablecloth restaurant that really was about quality casual fine dining. And it worked out that way because it grew and grew over the years, slowly but surely. Now, twenty-five years later, it's the joy of my life other than my two boys.

I couldn't be two places at once, and I couldn't clone myself, so it was really important to have someone I loved and trusted, as I did Jerry Baxter, watching over the show. However, it was not too long, about six years after we acquired Midtown, that Jerry surprised me; he said, "Randy, you know I watched my two children from my marriage with Emily grow up, but I was away at work so much that I never spent much time with them." He started talking about his young son, Timothy, who is my godson and was still a boy: "I want to be at home to be with him, to be a bigger part of his life than I was in Julian and Leslie's lives." I understood that, and I asked, "What are you trying to say, Jerry?" He said, "Well, I'm giving you my six-months' notice. And I want to give you time to figure out what you want to do going forward, but I really want to spend time with Mitzi and Timothy and enjoy my life. It's time for me to slow down and retire." Jerry's twelve years older than I am, and I understood where he was coming from because I'd always wanted to be a father. Fortunately, later in life I was blessed with two sons while still being owner of Sunset Grill and Cabana and Midtown Cafe.

Jerry's retirement transition ended up with Doug Stevenson being the general manager. I later hired Gina Kochevar (who's now been there 21 years.) Then a couple months after that, I hired Patrick Petzcko. Unfortunately, Patrick had some health issues during the first summer of Covid and was unable to return to work. But they were the core management team in the front of the house along with a lot of longtime employees like John Woodard and Mike Bassow.

After the great recession of 2008 and the flood of 2010, I started doing double duty between Sunset and Midtown. I'd work the door at Midtown for early lunch, 11:00 - around 12:30. Then I'd drive 2 miles over to Sunset and work the door for that crowd. That way I was visible at both places and tried to keep everybody happy. Then Sunset started slowing down and I was still too much in debt from opening Cabana in 2005 and Recession 2.0. After New Year's Eve on 2014, I closed the door on the Sunset Grill New Year's Day 2015. I knew I wouldn't be working that door anymore, so I took with me Paul Harmon's painting, "The Rainbow Man." I had always had a strong connection to that painting feeling it represented that part of me who liked to look beyond limits—beyond the rainbow. I hung it in the greeting area of Midtown where it remains and where I still work the door during weekdays.

I wasn't the only long-term Sunset family member who made the transition to Midtown. For example, Dale King, who started with me in 1989 at Moonbeams Restaurant as a server, came from Sunset Grill and now works at Midtown. John Woodard recently returned to the fold. It's inside information that we call Midtown "Sunset Village" and joke it's for all the older Sunset Grill employees who wanted to slow down the pace and avoid the super late hours of Sunset. That's true for the most part, but there are still times, especially during breakfast, brunch, and lunch, that get plenty busy. We all do our part and more to keep the store successful day and night. It takes a village to take care of Sunset Village, and I'm proud and thankful to be part of it

## HOW THE KITCHEN GOES

A wonderful thing happened along the way in the kitchens of both Sunset and Midtown. My friend, Chef Michael Tuohy of Atlanta, who was a James Beard nominee, decided to accept my invitation to move to Nashville and talk about developing a strategic partnership with me at both Sunset Grill and Midtown Cafe. Michael's a wonderful fellow, and we remain friends today. However, his wife, Patty, subsequently received a tremendous offer from Emory University in Atlanta, and Michael chose to go back to Atlanta to work in the restaurant business. He opened up Woodfire, which became a nationally acclaimed restaurant.

I have always felt, and feel to this day, that culinary talent is the key to a restaurant, and consistency, derived by good management and leadership in the kitchen, is critical. They're really the captain of the ship and how the kitchen goes, so goes the restaurant. So, when we acquired Midtown, we moved some people on the existing Sunset Grill staff over to the Midtown kitchen to complement the existing crew, and to learn and improve what they wanted to do. There were also initial dishes that I wanted to add along the way.

During Michael's time in Nashville, Chef Brian Uhl had joined the Sunset Grill. Chef Brian had worked with Craig Clifft at F. Scott's. Brian grew from sous chef to chef de cuisine at Sunset Grill and really was the hardest working culinarian I've ever worked with. From Queens, New York, he was hard-nosed and straightforward, and direct in his communications, which I liked and respected. I appreciated his honesty, and people enjoyed working with him. However, Brian was no easy pushover; he was someone who really earned my respect. So when Michael left, it was an easy choice for Brian to take over. Chef Brian also put his stamp on Midtown Cafe, at which point it really began to turn into something quite successful. Brian came on board in 1999, so around 2000 that transition began with Brian being more involved with Midtown Cafe as well as being the executive chef over at Sunset Grill.

As the transition evolved, we sent some different sous chefs over from Sunset to Midtown. Ultimately one of Brian's proteges, Max Pastor, who had joined us at Sunset Grill as a sous chef to open Cabana in 2005, came over to Midtown Cafe in 2007 as sous chef, and soon was promoted to chef and remains chef there today. Chef Max Pastor is the nicest, hardest-working person in the restaurant business that I've ever worked with. Brian was probably the hardest working, but Max is so much easier going, and so wonderful to work with, and a really caring person about his family and his work family at Midtown Cafe. Miguel Martinez had started as a dishwasher at Sunset Grill in 2000, and when we needed a dishwasher at Midtown, Brian moved him over. Miguel then grew into a prep person, and then into a line cook, and eventually became sous chef on days. Miguel has played an important role in the organization since 2000 and is Max's right hand. Miguel mar-ried Meg, the lady who worked on pantry, and they have two kids; they live 70 miles away, and he commutes five-days-a-week to Midtown Cafe.

A restaurant like Midtown is the sum of its parts, but all the parts have to get along and work well together, and that is part of the reason for Midtown's success through the years. Peo-ple who are long-term profes-sionals, who care about them-selves and what they do, and

*Chef Brian is remembered for his affectionate gestures.*

can get along with other people well, become part of a successful restaurant. People who don't get along and aren't comfortable in that environment or don't enjoy being in the restaurant business either in the front or back of the house soon find their way out the door because they just bring too much drama and too much uncertainty. You gotta love what you do and who you do it with, and that's the key to Midtown Cafe. We have a crew that really cares about each other and works together. (Randy Rayburn)

Painting by Sam Dunlap

# CHEF BRIAN UHL

## "THE ANSWER IS YES—WHAT IS THE QUESTION?"

When I interviewed Chef Brian Uhl, he was a partner in Cabana and Executive Chef of Cabana, Midtown Cafe, and the Sunset Grill. He slid into a booth at Cabana (oops! I mean a cabana at Cabana!) looking none the worse for wear for having just finished dinner prep. His white chef coat rested nonchalantly on his shoulders, covered his ample frame, and bore only a few food stains—nothing his easy manner and beaming smile did not make up for. We talked about food, friends, and the frantic nature of the kitchen. Regardless of his pleasant manner, Brian maintained the truth of his "cranky" reputation in the kitchen. Then again, as a premier chef responsible for three of the most popular and successful restaurants in Nashville, one must assume some discipline is necessary.

A restaurant kitchen is an intense environment: pans sizzle, pots boil, electronic timers beep, and dishwashers slam pots and pans. Over the top of the din, waiters loudly inquire about their customers' orders, and the chef and sous chefs shout instructions and answers. Regardless of the organized chaos, Brian was known for expecting full attention to the task at hand in the food preparation area. And that means—even for THAT young generation—not using a cell phone while working on the line. Brian is infamous for two extreme responses to line workers ignoring his "no cell phone rule": one phone went plunging into the deep freeze and another went plop into the deep fryer!

Brian's "fire and ice" approach is private Sunset family lore, but he was known nationally for his innovative use of regional foods in recipes for all three restaurants. Brian started using local foods early in his Nashville career and is remembered as a leader in the current movement of using regional foods and private suppliers in restaurants. Brian explained to me that he designed menus and recipes around seasonal produce and "things I enjoy." Two popular items that were featured at Cabana, Tennessee Catfish Sliders, and Sweet Potato Biscuits with Peach Preserves, showcased his sense of what his restaurant guests would enjoy.

Brian always said that his menu was "80% customer driven." Although Brian's training included classic French cuisine, and he had worked with famous chefs in New York and Germany, he stated "it is not realistic to put my ego in front of the customers." In addition to interesting and delicious food—he always considered cost: "People are looking for value and you have to give it to them." I could see that folks dining in any of the three restaurants would enjoy food planned and prepared by a chef who not only loves food, but also appreciates his guests. In terms of making his guests at all three restaurants happy Brian's mantra is "The answer is yes—what is the question?"

In 2016, Brian became ill while still in his prime, only 51. He underwent extensive treatment and even commuted back and forth from Atlanta, Georgia for medical therapy. Writer Chris Chamberlain with the *Nashville Scene* wrote that "rather than dwell on the uncertain future of his health, Chef Uhl decided to marshal the attention that his friends have been bestowing on him as they ask how they can help into a positive development with a fundraising event for the newly established Brian Uhl Culinary Scholarship at Nashville State Culinary Community College." Chamberlain contends that proof that Brian had maintained his well-known sense of humor was evident in the hashtag for the event: "#brianmakescancerhisbitch." Chamberlain continued: "Nashville's finest chefs gathered at the Cabana Restaurant on May 9th not only to raise funds for the scholarship, but also as a 'joyful tribute to celebrate Uhl.'"

The Sunset/Cafe Midtown family and Brian's wife, Cindy, lost Chef Brian on Tuesday, August 23, 2016.

Chef Brian Uhl is remembered for his expertise, but also for his ability and willingness to train new people interested in the food industry. The success at Midtown Cafe is one testament to Chef Brian's legacy. (Karren Pell)

# DALE KING

## "RANDY CAN BE A TOUGH COOKIE, BUT HE'S GOT A SOFT HEART."

### "SO MANY STORIES"

Dale likes to talk about the Sunset Grill days: "So many stories!" Dale met Randy in 1989 while they were both working at Moonbeams. Randy talked to Dale about plans to open his dream grill, and Dale told Randy to call him when that dream came true. As it happened, Dale was looking for a job when Randy called. "What 'cha doin'" Randy asked? "Waiting for you to call," Dale replied. And so Dale became part of the opening team for Sunset Grill. Dale worked at the Sunset Grill for a decade and then left to explore other worlds. Then he was invited to the Sunset Grill's fifteen-year anniversary party. Asked where he was working, he replied that if he was working he could not have come to the party, and so Randy hired him back on the spot for Midtown Cafe.

Randy is infamous for cramming in two tops to serve more customers. Dale remembers one time he was at a table taking an order and, when he was finished, he turned to head to the kitchen to turn in the orders but could not move as he had been penned in by two-tops while at his customer's table.

Dale liked to work out on the patio. He even liked to work the uncovered tables. The patio was known to leak, and Dale remembers serving customers and running an obstacle course to avoid the buckets set around the floor to catch water dripping from the patio roof. Well, Randy always says the show must go on! Dale recalls that one time there were so many leaks that there were only two dry areas on the patio. On one, tables had been pushed together in order to seat a large group of businessmen. Then, actress Sharon Stone showed up and wanted the other area. One of the businessmen recognized her and jumped up to go meet her. However, Dale asked him to please sit back down as it is Sunset Grill policy, and indeed Nashville tradition, to not bother celebrities. Stone noticed the gentleman and told Dale it was fine for the man to come over. It was a slow night and everyone in the kitchen was betting on what Stone would order. Most bets were on the more sophisticated dishes—steak, or seafood. But to everyone's surprise, she ordered a chicken pot pie. Another time while working on the patio, Dale looked up from the table he was helping and saw his truck go by—full of the kitchen staff joy riding with Lynda driving!

Dale also liked to work the front of the dining room. One Sunday night he recalls that singer-songwriter Lucinda Williams came in with an entourage including her producer. Tables were pushed together and drinks delivered. Then suddenly Lucinda became very vocal and carried on for about fifteen minutes cursing Nashville—Dale recalls the rant went along the lines of "Fuck this town and those skinny assed women in fancy clothes from stores on West End." Dale was in the kitchen when it started, but he immediately went out on the floor, and the funny part was that no one in the dining room was paying her any attention. Finally, she sat down and was quiet as suddenly as she had stood up and ranted. "Geez Lucinda," Dale told her, "you scared me. There for a minute I thought my ex wife had come in!" A scary memory involves the half wall that divided the dining room and a small hall that led to and from the kitchen. The half wall was topped by a wide ledge where Randy like to put decorative objects. One time a magnum, a large wine bottle, was creatively posed. Dale came out of the kitchen with a large tray and lost his balance as he turned to go into the dining room. Trying to correct himself, he clipped the magnum. With a huge noise, the bottle went sailing off the ledge and landed on a table full of customers! Luckily it didn't break and even more luckily, it didn't hurt anyone.

Other tales involve the other servers. Dale and Lynda were good friends and often played pranks on one another—especially during late night. One of his favorite pranks was to hide behind a door and jump out at her. She'd scream, "I hate you," and then chase him

14

through the dining room. One particular evening there was one piece of the dessert Neapolitan Bomb left—both Dale and Lynda had been eyeing it for hours. Then Dale walked into the kitchen and saw Lynda grab it. "Oh no you don't," he said, "you gotta give me a bit of that." But when he grabbed it, the ice cream got on her blouse. That made her mad, and so the chase was on. At one point, she chased Dale through the kitchen, and, as she raced by, she picked up a small bowl of tomatoes. Dale ran out the back door and down the street. But Lynda followed and lobbed the tomatoes at him one by one. Dale said he had to stand on the street for a few minutes wondering when it would be safe for him to go back in and see to his tables.

Halloween was always a wild night as servers dressed up in costumes and a party vibe prevailed. One year, Dale dressed up like Randy—he wore some suspenders and folded up a tablecloth for a little extra midriff weight. But the crowning glory of the costume was that Dale's entire head was covered by a pumpkin head. Everybody loved the costume—including Randy. All night along Randy introduced "the pumpkin head" to customers as "another Randy." When Dale went to wait on tables, customers would exclaim, "Oh! We got the pumpkin head!"

Halloween wasn't the only wild night. Dale remembers that some nights it took a long time to clean up, wrap silver, do chores. After finally finishing, he and Lynda and maybe a couple others would sit at the bar and have some beers. Suddenly—there was Marilyn—the daytime bartender! Her arrival meant it was early morning—the night had flown and there they were still at the bar. Marilyn would chase them off—"You're not supposed to be here—go home!"

The vibe at Midtown Cafe is calmer. Dale explains, "We're all getting older—we're just not as wild." Still, a good deal of camaraderie exists among both staff and regular customers. Dale said, "it was so good to see everybody after the pandemic lockdown. Sometimes I'd be missing certain regular customers and thinking of them and look up and they'd be walking in; it was great to see them."

## DALE'S MIDTOWN CAFE FAVES

**MEDITERRANEAN PASTA**
With Angel Hair, Roasted Roma Tomatoes, Fresh Spinach, Artichoke Hearts, and Mushrooms Tossed with Basil Pesto

**GRILLED SALMON**
On a Bed of Domestic Mushroom Risotto with Grilled Asparagus and Sun-dried Tomato Ragout

Dale recalls he survived many of Randy's infamous line-up speeches. Dale just got used to the rant and knew Randy had another side. Dale said during lock down, Randy took care of the staff—made sure they could pay their bills and were okay, "Randy can be a tough cookie, but he's got a soft heart." In the over twenty-five years Dale has worked for Randy, he knows both sides! Dale says the staff is happy at Midtown and that vibe (plus yummy entrees from the Sunset Grill plus fabulous new dishes) contributes to make Midtown Cafe the comfortable enjoyable eatery that it is. (Karren Pell)

# DOUG STEVENSON

**"I'M THE LAST OF THE STAFF WHO WAS WORKING HERE [MIDTOWN] BEFORE RANDY."**

**"I'M PROUD TO SERVE GOOD FOOD AND WORK WITH GOOD PEOPLE."**

Doug remembers that Randy taking over Midtown was quiet. So quiet that even the staff didn't know it was happening. Doug was working on what turned out to be last night under old management. The previous owner was known to be very conservative and worked within a tight budget. But that night, he was hosting a large table, and was ordering good wine and high-end entrees. People around the table were toasting and acting in a celebratory mode—Doug felt like something was up. He saw John go to kitchen and heard him announce that the restaurant had been sold;

John did not tell the wait staff. So on first work day, Monday, Doug was there early to see "what was going on." The staff was assembled and told the news.

Doug says the menu, environment, and working conditions are all improved since Randy took over. Doug has stayed the whole time; he is the only one of the original staff that remains. But he says it was not trauma dramas that caused servers to leave–just life changes. Doug notes that the situation is always evolving. When times start going down, such as during the pandemic lockdown, Randy figures out a way for them to go up.

Doug says he has stayed and because he is proud to serve good food and happy to work with good people. Doug loves food and so it works for him that Randy is a stickler about food. The menu has evolved; Randy tweaks it continuously; it has changed drastically from original. Some of the changes were Chef Brian Uhls' signature dishes. Chef Brian was executive chef of all three restaurants running at one time-Sunset Grill, Cabana, and Midtown Cafe. The Lobster "Mac and Cheese" was one of Chef Brian Uhl's popular recipes. The Lemon Artichoke Soup is retained from the previous owner's menu. It is John Petrocelli's wife's family recipe, and Randy had to purchase the rights to the soup at the same time he purchased Midtown Cafe. *Bon Appétit* wanted the recipe for Lemon Artichoke Soup and Randy refused.

Doug says he suggests different entrees to his guests on different nights. Doug often pushes the lamb, but other perennial faves are the Lobster "Mac and Cheese" with sea scallops, and lemon artichoke soup. Doug says if the folks are not from the south, he is duty bound to suggest the shrimp and grits–a classic southern dish made to perfection at Midtown Cafe. In fact, the staff went to Charleston for a learning trip and sampled shrimp and grits at some of the four-star and five-star restaurants in the Queen City. Doug was proud to say he preferred Midtown's version to any of those served. Midtown's Shrimp and Grits features blackened shrimp tossed with bacon, mushroom, tomatoes, and scallions served in stone ground smoked Gouda cheese grits.

Doug works as a server and general manager. He is committed to Midtown Cafe as it is his livelihood. However, he is also an established visual artist working in clay. He has two degrees–one in education and one in fine arts. Doug has taught students ages 6-13 at Watkins, an established art school summer camp, for 18 years. He sometimes hears from some of his students who have grown and gone on to get their fine arts degrees. He had a teaching position but found the bureaucracy confining. For example, his principal required detailed minute by minute lesson plans. She would enter his room and check to see if the class was "on time" per his plans with activities; no regard for the "teachable moment." Although at times he is working long hours both teaching and working at Midtown, he says he likes it and prefers not to rely on teaching as his main income.

Doug can tell great stories about celebrities. For a while he was the Midtown Cafe representative for a Nashville program called "Eats"–that was a food tour. A bus would stop in front of restaurant at an appointed time, and the tour's participants would be treated to a small amount of an entrée like a small cup of Lemon Artichoke Soup. Then

Doug would tell a story about a celebrity visiting Midtown—he laughs that "everybody loves celebrities!" Doug noted that in Nashville culture, celebrities are allowed to dine without interruption or fanfare. Nonetheless, many personalities enjoy and even want to be recognized. Randy Travis, for example, enjoys being recognized; he calls many of the staff by name. John Schneider, the actor who played Bo in Dukes of Hazzard, also enjoys being recognized. One afternoon Doug was going into work and noticed a man bending over his car—a Porsche. As Doug got closer, he recognized Schneider, a frequent patron. Doug quipped, "Well, John, who else would be out here working on a car?" Many celebrities are so comfortable and pleased with the staff and food that they are frequent guests at Midtown. While working in Nashville, Robert Redford was a frequent patron. Reba McEntire is a frequent guest and often even drives herself. Doug told a fun story about Neil Armstrong. Armstrong was a speaker at a Vanderbilt conference, and he and several other men were dining at Midtown. The others guests, as well as Doug, were mesmerized by Neil's stories. Another Neil, Neil Young, was recording in Nashville and a member of his staff called Midtown to make a reservation with a requirement—a table for ten and must be out in an hour and half. They were assured that would happen. Neil and his group arrived and ordered a large amount and wide variety of entrees and entire courses accompanied by lots of red wine. Doug said the kitchen staff was ready and the dishes came flying out of the kitchen one after another. Neil and his guests loved the food and wine and were done easily within the time constraint. Kiefer Sutherland recorded a country album in Nashville and enjoyed having dinner at Midtown to the extent that he became a regular during his stays. After Kiefer ate, he would ask, "Hey Doug, are you finished?" and if Doug was, Sutherland would say, "Grab some wine on my tab and sit down here with me and talk." Many celebrities know wait staff and Randy by name. The staff knows their names and makes sure they are treated the way they want to be treated. The best story featured Dolly Parton. Dolly came in and sat down at a table and ordered dinner. As previously stated, it is the custom not to bother known personalities. However, this particular evening a child with some challenges noticed her. Seems he was a huge fan and became very excited to see her. The child's mother asked Doug if there was any way the little boy could meet Dolly. Doug told the child's mother he would approach Dolly about meeting the child. Doug told Dolly the situation, apologizing for interrupting her privacy. But Dolly was thrilled to meet the little boy. She jumped up from her seat and went over to the child's table. Hugs, photos, and general joy was abundant.

## DOUG'S MIDTOWN CAFE FAVES

**MIDTOWN'S SHRIMP AND GRITS**
Features Blackened Shrimp Tossed with Bacon, Mushrooms, Tomatoes, and Scallions served in Stone Ground Smoked Gouda Cheese Grits

Doug smiles and laughs easily, and it is easy to surmise that Dolly Parton does not have to be present for joy and fun to appear at Midtown Cafe—Doug is very capable of spreading his own version of joy—along with some Lobster "Mac and Cheese!" (Karren Pell)

# GEMMA FREIDLI

## "I'M NON-STOP."   "IT'S ALL GOOD."

Gemma has been working in the restaurant industry since she was fourteen-year-old, and has been working with Randy for thirteen years. She met Randy while she was working at the Cabana Restaurant. Cabana was Randy's third restaurant adventure and was located kinda sorta catty-cornered across from the Sunset Grill. After lunch rush Randy would come over to see Cabana Manager and partner Craig Clifft. Gemma recalls, "Experiences with Randy were always good. He'd come in and ask, 'Hey Kid, how's Clifft treating you?'" Nonetheless, Gemma was aware of, as she puts it, "the intimidating side" of Randy's personality, which inspired her to "spend the first three years on my toes."

Gemma is currently the day manager and server at Midtown Cafe, working closely with Tricia Bassow and Kristie Rickard while Randy helps them run the door. Ryan Duke,

*Left to Right: Ryan Duke and Amanda Gamble*

Gina's daughter, and Amanda Gamble run the door at night while Doug Stevenson and Gina Kochevar manage the restaurant and Dale King, who has been with Randy since 1989, keeps things interesting.

During the pandemic, Gemma remembers that Randy "touched base and was good to my boys. Randy is like a father figure." As others often say, Gemma says, "When you get to know Randy, he has a helluva heart to him."

Gemma loves the Midtown menu explaining it's, "Hard not to rave about the menu." She has a lot of regular customers. She laughs and says they come in, get the same menu items, sit in the same seats, same tables. Gemma is a favorite among the regular customers, but one pair earned a favorite place in her fave customer list. The story begins the first time they came in and Gamma was their server. They were a young couple from California; they had a great time and showed up again about a month and a half later. Gamma, in her own special way, recognized them and welcomed them back. They also remembered her, and said they were glad she was there and would be their server. Gemma recalls, "They were celebrating something, but they didn't volunteer, and I didn't intrude." After they finished eating, Gemma completed their bill transaction and left the paper receipt on the table. When she noted they had left, she went over to

pick up the receipt and was totally shocked to see they had left a beautiful note and a $1000 tip. Gemma recalls, "I was ready to cry in front of the whole restaurant." She ran out to thank them, but they were gone.

Gemma describes herself as, "I'm non-stop—one of those people who some folks might say in the early morning—could you dial it down a notch?" Gemma loves her job, and the other servers, and her customers. She says Randy is, "family." Like many people who work in Nashville these days, Gemma lives outside of the city in Clarksville with her two boys. So, in addition to a long day on her feet, she has a daily commute. But, as Gemma says, "It's all good." (Karren Pell)

# GINA KOCHEVAR

**"WE'VE HAD SOME CHARACTERS COME THROUGH HERE."**
**"I LOVE THE PEOPLE I WORK WITH."**

I haven't spent as much time with the staff at Midtown as I did with the Sunset family during my songwriter days. But when I visit Nashville, I always meet Jerry and Suzanne at Midtown for brunch. We like to sit at that little table near the front window. On my way to Midtown Cafe the image that comes to mind is Gina's big glasses, Gina's big smile, and Gina giving me a big glass of champagne. So how do you beat that?

Gina went to work for Randy in May 2002 as a Midtown Cafe server and bartender. She remembers that Jerry had just retired, and she had a fun crew to work with. She knew Tricia Basson and some other staff members who had previously worked for Faison's and 12th & Porter. Gina says, "I love the people I work with-some come and go. I remember working with Tricia, Doug, Mike Wyatt, Patrick, Molly, Paul Neil;" Gina recalls with a laugh, "We've had some characters come through here." Gina also says, "Randy is good to me—longest job I've ever had."

When the Covid pandemic hit, Midtown Cafe shut down. Gina said, "The first month was okay; the second month was hard; when I got the call to reopen, I was ready." During the time Midtown was shut down, she said regular customers did what they could to support the staff by buying gift cards and giving generous tips. When the Midtown first reopened, it could not offer service to the previous number of tables, so Randy only had three servers to start who would come back to work. Gina said, "I worked really hard—sometimes 70 hours a week, during that time. But I was happy to be here, happy to have a job, and now we are busier than ever."

Gina loves her regular customers. One couple, Charlie Talent and his wife, come in at least twice a week for lunch. Gina says they are "super nice, generous, and treat people with kindness." Gina remembers another customer who came in three or four times a week. He always ordered the Caesar Salad with Blackened Salmon and liked "about 50 sweet and lows in his iced tea."

Gina has several dishes she is partial to, "the veal dishes have stood the test of time." One time she recalls she was working on a shuttle night—when food is taken out to guests riding to downtown venues and stopping at restaurants—and she accidentally spilled the veal piccata sauce all over one lady. Luckily, Gina recalls, "she was nice about it. We definitely had a dry-cleaning bill on that one."

In addition to her regular customers, Gina recalls having some celebrities as guests. Working at the bar one day, Gina looked up and Dolly Parton was coming from the ladies room area and beckoned to Gina, "Honey," Dolly said, "your toilet is not working, but its okay I just peed." Gina said she waited on Robert Plant, "I was a little star struck." Neil Young visited Midtown Cafe several times—sometimes with friends, sometimes by himself at the bar. One of Gina's favorites was Kiefer Sutherland: "He was staying across the street for two weeks. He was a really good guy—funny and kind."

## GINA'S MIDTOWN CAFE FAVES

### VEAL PICCATA
Sautéed in Butter with White Wine, Lemon Juice and Capers Served with Fresh Herb Buttered Angel Hair Pasta

### VEAL OSCAR
Scallopini Topped with Fresh Lump Crab Meat and Asparagus Served with Bearnaise Sauce and Fresh Garden Vegetable Risotto

### VEAL SALTIMBOCCA
Layered with Benton's Tennessee Ham, Provolone Cheese and Fresh Sage Served over Yukon Mashed Potatoes and Fried Spinach with a Red Wine Sauce

And if you can't decide...

### VEAL 3 WAYS
A Tasting of the Piccata, Oscar, and Saltimbocca

Gina has a quick and fun laugh. She is good at her job, and I'm sure everyone feels like I do when I'm at Midtown that she is glad to see them and loves waiting on them. But sometimes I like to think it's just me. (Karren Pell)

# JERRY BAXTER

## "WISH GRANTED"

When Jerry Baxter talks about the adventures during his early years working with Randy, he laughs, "Had we been sober we would be able to remember." Jerry and Randy were co-conspirators before the Sunset Grill opened. They share a long list of friends and acquaintances in Nashville whose affiliations run from politics, government, and charity work and, of course, other restaurateurs.

They met at the well-established restaurant, Sperry's. During their bachelor days, Jerry was part of the gang who lived at Randy's Tudor style house known as "Squirrel Hill"—so named, Jerry explains, because of the "All of the squirrels outside in the trees and all of the squirrels in the house." The "orphan" Thanksgivings, and other parties

*Above left to right: Randy with Jerry Baxter and the Best of the Best 5 Star Diamond Award*

hosted at Squirrel Hill have passed into Nashville folklore. I met Jerry at one of those fabled events.

Jerry and I first worked together at the fabled restaurant, The Third Coast. The Third Coast was located on the ground floor of an apartment house built in the early 1900s. Later, the establishment became a hotel known as "The Rock' n' Roll Hotel." Legend had it that Elvis had stayed at the Rock-'n'- Roll Hotel. Lodging was upstairs, and a bar and restaurant occupied the ground floor. By the time I knew it, the upstairs rooms were small apartments. The building's distressed brick structure stood three stories high, and guests reached the upper levels by a narrow stairway. It was like the place had two personalities or lived two lives: there was the upstairs reality where people lived, and the downstairs where people lived it up. Across a huge outdoor pebbledash patio, grown trees sheltered large, round tables. The patio was one of the most popular spots in town; waits could exceed three hours. Any one table seated a large party, but

Birthday gathering—all born on the same day but with different vintages: (left to right) Jerry Baxter, Dano Goosetree, Ernie Paquette, Randy Rayburn.

guests pulled chairs from all around the patio and then pulled the big tables together for even bigger parties. Wait staff, kitchen staff, bartender—all of us—busted our butts for hours getting drinks and food out to people more concerned with seeing and being seen than eating, but everyone was concerned with drinking. Jerry was floor manager, and I was hostess. He used to wear these white shorts and I wore short denim skirts, and we both wore white tennis shoes. Those were the days, my friends. We were cool, no doubt about it! We saw it all at the Third Coast: singers, songwriters, publishers, drug dealers, the famous, the infamous, and the wanna-bes, past and present. I met Dickie Betts, Wynonna Judd, and Paul Davis there. Legendary songwriter Harlan Howard held court on the sofas next to the bar. Ralph Murphy and his entourage usually required the more spacious accommodations of a table on the patio or, in the winter, in one of the back rooms with a fireplace. The guests were not the only known personalities—the staff also had a reputation. The bar was tended by our best bud, Dano. Rusty and Stretch waited tables. Beautiful Louise Phillips, who later married Ralph Murphy, was another hostess. One time I saw Rusty walk up to a double table full of people at about 1:00 in the morning, put a burgundy napkin on his head and announce to them all: "Hello! I'm your waiter Rusty. I am your connection to the kitchen and the bar. Fuck with me and you get nuthin!!" Yep, like the song said, "Oh Baby, Baby it's a wild world."

When Randy was planning to open the Sunset Grill, Jerry was one of the first people he put on his "must have" list. Jerry knew that Randy had sold Squirrel Hill to raise the capital to open the Sunset Grill; his respect for Randy's sacrifice and his own attachment to the Sunset family gave him a dim view of other less invested employees. One of Sunset Team's favorite memories involves Jerry's decision regarding a hostess. I was working in the office at that time, and was frantically finishing running off the menus when the phone rang. I remember thinking "I'm coming with the blame menus!!" I jerked up the phone and heard Jerry say, "I need you down here now." Well, that was rather strange. But I asked no questions, grabbed the menus, and quickly walked the block to the restaurant. Now, we all knew the hostess had been under-enthusiastic for some time. She was always whining about something: her hours, her schedule, her tips—her boyfriend! Seems that morning she walked through the door with a particularly dark countenance. Jerry greeted her, but her only response was "I wish I did not have to be here." Although the lunch rush was due any minute (and the menus were late!), and she was scheduled as the only hostess, Jerry magnanimously responded, "Wish granted!" and sent her home for good: thus the call to the office. When he told me what happened, I was glad to work the door. That is the way it always worked—Team Sunset pitched in, the menus got run, guests seated, lunch served. We all agreed that we would much rather work harder than have someone in our midst who was not happy to be a part of Team Sunset.

Jerry is instrumental in fulfilling wishes of another kind—he is the chief organizer and founder of "Soup Sunday." The family event, which recently observed its twenty-fifth year, benefits Our Kids. The organization's website reads, "Help. Hope. Healing. For Children and Families Affected by Child Sexual Abuse." A horrible and sad problem in our time, but Jerry and the Nashville restaurant community do more than lament. On Soup Sunday over fifty participating restaurants ladle up a variety of delicious soups—many of which are mainstays for their specific culinary corner. The fun day is always scheduled for the last Sunday in February, and in addition to soup, there is a soup judging contest, a huge silent auction, celebrity sightings, and door prizes. People happily stand in lines a block long to get a tray of small cups containing tasty soups. It is THE place to be and be seen. And there is plenty to see: prestigious chefs serving as judges, popular emcees keeping a steady music/info stream stirred up, radio personalities giving more than a dash of cleverness, and television and recording stars adding that special ingredient that only they can provide. Over two hundred volunteers help with crowd control, each restaurant has a small staff to help serve, and then there are the over 1500 guests. In 2014, over $150,000 was raised. That kind of cash can help to make a few good wishes come true.

For a while Jerry was operating partner of Midtown Cafe. These days he is retired, but make no mistake, he remains an integral part of the Sunset/Midtown family. In fact, you might see him at Midtown any time, but if you do, just be careful if he can hear what you wish for! (Karren Pell)

*Jerry Baxter accepting an award for his contributions to Soup Sundays.*

# JOHN WOODARD

**"IT'S REWARDING; I LOVE IT."**
**"THE CREW HAS A WAY WITH BREAKFAST."**

John worked as a full-time server at the Sunset Grill 1994-1998; when Craig and Randy opened Midtown Cafe, John became a manager at Sunset. Then he moved to Midtown as management from 1999 to 2001.

After 2001, John left the Sunset-Midtown family and tried some other realities including moving to Colorado. In all, he was out of the restaurant business for nearly twenty years.

John and his wife moved back to Nashville, and one fine Saturday in 2021 came into Midtown for brunch. John and his wife sat at table #34 and talked to Doug. Doug happily mentioned that he often made $400-$500 as server for breakfast and lunch. John said that piece of information made an impression, and four days later he came in and talked to Randy. Randy was glad to see him, but told John there were no management positions available. John said," What if I put on my blacks?" And Randy said, "Just let me know what you want your schedule to be."

Describing his favorite foods at Midtown, John says, "It's beautiful when it goes out. It's fun to serve all day. The crew has a way with breakfast. "

Looking back, John says he has "Lots of fond memories here. I have been fortunate to work with professional staff through the years." He recalls late nights at the Sunset that ran into the mornings: "We'd still be sitting at the bar, and Marilyn (daytime manager) would show up and exclaim, 'You guys get out of here!'"

Another fun Sunset memory happened while John was working as a server on the patio. He was explaining the evening specials to guests on table 82 on a Friday night about 8:00. While talking, he noticed a limo parked, but idling without a driver. Then suddenly, John saw a guy, who obviously had more than his share of alcohol, hop in the limo and try to do a turn. In the process, he wrecked the limo and tore into three parked cars. He then jumped out of car and took off running. John, young and bold, told his customers, "Excuse me—I'll be right back." He then jumped over the brick wall of the patio and tackled the guy against the chain link fence of the post office. John held him there until someone else came to help, and then the police came. When John returned, the whole patio erupted into cheering. John laughs, "If I tried that now I'd pull something in my leg, but I was 35 and could do anything!"

Besides car thieves—John recalls that the Sunset Grill really was "the place to see and be seen." John recalls serving celebrities like Keith Urban and Nicole Kidman, George Strait, and Garth Brooks. John says, "They were not treated any differently—not bugged; celebrities could come into the Sunset Grill and feel at home. " John recalled that Uma Thurman "showed up barefooted. She sat at table 78 on the patio, ordered three appetizers, 2 bottles of chardonnay (and one to go), left, and tipped me $100. She was in and then gone in 45 minutes."

John loves working at Midtown, describing it as "Coming back home." Musing further John says, "Returning to being a server was not a choice I could have conceived right before I made the decision. But I do not consider it any way a step back. The challenge is the physical demands of the job: My body is different than 20 years ago, and that adjustment was the hardest part. But it's like a switch that flips and then I'm 'on.'" John only works days: "I get a groove going—I'm up at 5:00, at work by 7:00. By 8:15 the restaurant is full and everybody is crankin'. I work a double. Then, after lunch, I do side duties and go home to spend time with family and dogs. It's rewarding. I love it." (Karren Pell)

## JOHN'S MIDTOWN CAFE FAVES

### NASHVILLE PIGS IN A BLANKET
Two Biscuits with MILD BBQ Dry Rub Roasted Pork Tenderloin served with Two Eggs Any Way and sides of Alabama White Sauce and Country Sausage Gravy

# MAX PASTOR

## "I'M HAPPY IF THE GUEST IS HAPPY."

Chef Brian hired Max Pastor as a sous chef and part of opening team for the Cabana in 2005. Max then switched to Midtown Cafe in 2007. Max drives 25 miles one way to work every day from Gallatin, TN. Living outside of Nashville but working in Nashville is not unusual because in the last decade real estate values have skyrocketed. Max says the schools are great and he and his family (wife, two girls and two boys) are comfortable there. Max says he is "blessed and lucky that he has had a job to support my family for 17 years."

Max has enjoyed the switch to fine dining. Although he mainly worked at Cabana, and since 2007 at Midtown, he pulled double duty the last few months of Sunset (2014) by supervising and assisting at Sunset and Midtown. He recalls that the last night, New Year's Eve, at Sunset was extremely busy. Max remembers that "A great memory for me is working with Chef Brian—he is the one I consider my mentor. Gave me a chance to a be a good chef." Max was main chef for a few months; after Chef Brian died, Randy gave Max the title Executive Chef at Midtown Cafe in 2016.

Max says "I like to be consistent—to make food consistent. I like it when people are happy." One night a server came back to the kitchen and told Max one of the guests was so happy with the food that she "wanted to kiss him." That wasn't going to happen; Max prefers to remain, "backstage" in the restaurant business, but Max says "I am happy if the guest is happy. "

Max recalls a couple of celebrity stories. His favorite is when Don Henley came into the Midtown Cafe. It was toward the end of closing, and Max was going on vacation, so he was ready for his workday to be ended. However, when the server told him Don Henley wanted to order Max was excited. He remembered the Eagles from when he was young and listening to music with his uncle. Then Henley ordered off menu! He wanted a hamburger with blue cheese on top. Max's response—no problem! Max also remembers servers mentioned that Robert Plant, Steve Martin, and Linda Carter (Wonder Woman) were guests. However, Max says he and the servers never bother the celebrities—it is not polite or professional. Max also is also glad that David Schneider, who played "Bo" in the television show, Dukes of Hazzard, is a regular at Midtown. Max recalls when he was a kid, he used to watch the show and enjoyed it a lot. Sometimes he will go home and tell his children of a special celebrity encounter like, "Hey, today I fixed a hamburger with blue cheese on it for Don Henley!"

## MAX'S MIDTOWN CAFE FAVES

### SPINACH AND CHIPOTLE HUMMUS
An In-house Recipe Served with Crispy Grilled Pita and Topped with Feta Cheese

### CRISPY BRUSSELS SPROUTS
Tossed with Honey Lime Vinaigrette with Apples, Candied Walnuts, Mandarin Oranges, and Tennessee White Cheddar Cheese

When the restaurant closed during the pandemic lock down, Max was very worried. He now says he is very thankful that Midtown Cafe is recovering. He notes that brunch is a big part of that recovery, and the kitchen staff keep very busy during that shift. The dishes are dependably delicious—a credit to Max's hard work and focus on consistency.

Max is humble and proud of his work at Midtown Cafe: "Randy and I built our work relationship for 6 years—it is an honor to work for such a person-a professional who takes care of his people. And working for Chef Brian—if it wasn't for him, I wouldn't be here." Guests and Servers alike are happy that Chef Max is at Midtown Cafe. (Karren Pell)

# MIGUEL MARTINEZ

## "LEARNING SOMETHING MAKES YOU EXCITED."

Miguel Martinez has worked for Randy for 22 years. He started as a dishwasher at the Sunset Grill. His work ethic caught the attention of Chef Brian and in two months Miguel was in training to cook in the pantry section. Miguel believes that "If you want to move up, you gotta learn and work hard to do it." Miguel wanted to learn about grilling. He says that Chef Brian told him to "pay attention when given instructions," and Miguel notes that the other sous chefs in the kitchen "had a lot of patience."

Miguel later went to work at Midtown as a cook and then as a sous chef and therefore was not working at the Sunset's last day. Miguel remains interested in food preparation: "I like to learn more and more. Learning something makes you excited." He drives now 70 miles each day one-way to work.

Miguel says that he liked working in the "big and best kitchen at the Sunset Grill," but the "smaller kitchen at Midtown is really good." It worked out for him as he met his wife, Meg, who was working in the pantry then, and they now have two boys.

Miguel says some people might talk about problems, but "I'm focused on the food." Miguel says working at Midtown "is perfect for me, and that's why I keep working for Randy. I feel like this is my home." (Karren Pell)

Painting by Sam Dunlap

# SUNSET GRILL STORIES

In deciding to put together the business plan of the Sunset Grill in 1990, I found that Nashville was very open to the idea of American restaurants, and what was being called California cuisine or American cuisine in California. Having traveled the wine country in California and Oregon, I really liked some of the great restaurants in Napa Valley. I really enjoyed "Mustards" and probably looked at "Mustards" as one of the best examples that I emulated in my designing of Sunset Grill. By design I mean, not in terms of stagecraft, but what American restaurants were about: a nice clean stagecraft combined with some local American ingredients using English and American terms for food coming from American gardens—not using French terms for American products. That change extended to ingredients—for example, using grouper instead of imported sole or Scottish salmon. People were being made aware of American cuisine thanks to Alice Waters, (California chef, activist, restaurateur, and author, who is credited with the innovation of "California cuisine"), and its popularity was on the rise. In the past, American restaurants had copied the experience of Italian, German, Greek, and French restaurants. American cuisine was rising as an experience, and its own form of nationalism and pride in what we do here.

In the first part of 1990, Nashville was experiencing growth in spite of tight overall economic conditions. I asked my friend, Houston Thomas (co-owner of Sperry's—a well established restaurant in Belle Meade), about when is a good time to open a restaurant. He responded : "There are no good times to open a restaurant. In good times there is lots of competition. In bad times, restaurants go under, but if you survive through the tough times, then when the tide in the economic harbor comes back in, you will rise with the rest of the ships and go on." I decided it was time to do that so I sold my home of 12 years, Squirrel Hill Manor, and put all my chips on the table looking for a location to lease.

I signed the lease in early September on a building across the street from Faison's that was, at that time, a bicycle shop. I then worked with architectural designer Manuel Zeitlin and artist Paul Harmon. I hired David Criner (Criner Brothers Enterprises), and we gutted the building to have a clear canvas to create the Sunset Grill.

We added an open-air pebble-patio made from brown river gravel from the Cumberland River. At first there was no roof, and the sides were the low brick wall and brick pillars that inspired the nickname "Sun Henge." I had run out of funds, so Criner agreed to be paid weekly for work that remained to be done. When we opened, we attempted to coral the drinkers out to the patio, but everybody loved the patio—diners and drinkers.

So, working day and night, we finished the construction of the dining area, a small kitchen, the bar, and the patio in 41 days and opened November 20, 1990.

I wanted a separated bar from the dining area as I felt people wanted to hide a little bit. Manuel's architectural drawings featured a bar in the center of the restaurant. I had to hire another architect to get the bar in the corner of the building. I explained to Manuel, "You know design, but I know restaurants." In addition to Criner, we hired a crew of Vanderbilt carpenters who came in to work around 3:30 or 4:00 after their day job at Vanderbilt. Working with Dano, Jay Pennington, and Rusty Dunn we designed a beautiful bar that hung from the ceiling. We had to go vertical as there wasn't much space. We ended up with six booths, 15 bar stools, and a wait station around a multi-sided bar. Dano always told me that we built beautiful bars, but then I screwed them up by offering fifty or sixty wines by the glass.

I wanted an American restaurant and an American wine list. I believed that customers wanted options and would order what they wanted instead of what the host liked. I wanted to offer California and Washington State and Oregon wines. We didn't have a lot of money, but we could buy a bottle at a time and get more—even the very next day. I had worked at Opryland and opened the Jack Daniel's Saloon & Rhett's in 1983 which was an "All American menu" and offered the first all American wine list in Tennessee and possibly the southeast.

In my quest for an all-American wine list, there's an interesting story about Lipman Brothers Distributors. The sales representative from Lipman Brothers Distributors showed up one day and told me that I had to give them 50% of my wine list, or I got no discount on my wine purchases. I felt this was unreasonable, and I'd had some issues with

Lipman from my time at F. Scott's. I told the representative, "Bob, I've been laboring under the perception that I'm the customer, and you are here to serve my needs—not visa versa. I want to introduce you to my delete button. I've just deleted every one of your wines that I was going to carry, and I will never ever carry a product from your wine list." He didn't believe me. I invited him to the opening night party. I welcomed him, and his boss, Robert Lipman, who apologized. I said, "We'll see how my experiment (the American wine list) works out. But I guarantee I will never ever buy another bottle of wine from Lipman." He apologized again, and I agreed to talk in a year. A year later we were the hottest new restaurant in Nashville. I did finally buy some wine from Lipman. But he had realized that I had to carry their Jack Daniel's, but I didn't have to carry their wine.

 I designed the menu and recruited Richard Vaughn, who had been sous chef at F. Scott's under Chef Anita Hartel. We worked together, weighed a list of options of things we had done at F. Scott's, and came up with a menu we planned to expand later as we grew.

In addition to a place, food, and wine I had to have staff. I began hiring a core of an opening crew—I cherry picked from friends and people I'd worked with before. Dale King, Troy Van Atta, Suzanne Coleman, Robynne Napier, LeAnne Merrick, Kathy Davis, Rusty Dunn, Dano Goosetree, Ben Paty (Grill & Fish specialist), and Chef Richard Vaughn (from F. Scott's) rounded out the main crew.

We opened "The Grill of My Dreams" Thanksgiving week, November 20, 1990. We had a good opening crowd, but not huge, and that was good because it gave us a little time to get ready. On Thanksgiving we were closed, and Barry Pendley, who had worked with Jay Pennington and Baresco Restaurant Equipment, and I were installing shelving. Barry went and bought us turkey and dressing and the fixings from O'Charley's, and we took a break and sat down at one of the tables and had Thanksgiving dinner.

My public relations firm I had hired, MP & F's David Fox, persuaded Tom Lee from Chanel 4 WSMV to do a story on the difficulty of opening a restaurant in a recession, and it attracted a lot of attention. Over the weekend crowds increased, and by Monday after Thanksgiving there were lines at the door and two hour waits. It was like manna from Heaven. We added staff and worked day and night with what we had. The bookkeeper, Leann Merrick, made her office at booth 51 in the bar. Later I made space for an office in the house I had rented a block from the restaurant. Waits and lines and an overwhelmed kitchen blissfully continued through the holiday season.

And then history intervened. The bombing of Baghdad began on January 17, 1991. Americans were transfixed on CNN's 24-hour coverage—viewers watched the beginnings of a war for the first time on live television. Journalist Wolf Blitzer's coverage made him famous; Bernard Shaw, John Holliman, and Peter Arnet became household words when they refused to leave prior to the bombing and reported from a Baghdad hotel during the bombing. Americans were mesmerized and worried and did not leave their homes. Sunset Grill was the last thing on their minds. Then, bombing stopped in thirty days; war began and ended 6 days later. When the news coverage of the war stopped, the crowds came back to the Sunset Grill immediately to celebrate.

Spring came early—right after Desert Storm—and the Happy Hour dinner crowd flooded the restaurant. Lines and two hour waits returned. We had survived the five weeks of Desert Storm, and we were going and blowing. One year later we were the hottest new restaurant in Nashville. (Randy Rayburn)

## THE PATIO

Everybody loved the Sunset Grill patio. When the Sunset Grill first opened, funds were tight and even the simple patio had a zero budget; there was only dirt from building to sidewalk. However, construction boss extraordinaire, Dave Criner, agreed to be paid back weekly, and so when opening day came there was an open-air patio.

The patio in its first phase was a pebble floor, open air structure with a brick half wall and brick columns that were ten feet high. Staff called it "Sun Henge." The original plan was to move drinkers from the small bar to the patio, but the patio was so popular that it grew to include diners for lunch and dinner. The patio's popularity created an immediate problem. During lunch and dinner rush, there was no room inside to handle diners from the patio if inclement weather suddenly arrived; obviously a rainstorm produced chaos. Suzanne remembers Randy walking around the block and staring into the sky as if he could will the rain away. Given the popularity of the patio, and the increased number of tables generating revenue the patio created, Randy decided some kind of covering was important.

The second phase featured patio umbrellas donated by liquor wholesalers. When the season changed, and umbrellas were no longer needed, propane heaters were rolled in to keep guests warm and thus prevented laying off staff.

The third phase brought in a permanent retractable roof. One section of the patio

remained open. A motor on each end of the roofed section, and four-by-four windows allowed the patio to be enclosed and yet have a feeling of being open. In nice weather, the roof was rolled back, and the entire patio was open.

Most guests did not notice it, but there were a few little bumps regarding the patio. First of all, the motor that closed or opened the roof sounded like the hatch on the Starship Enterprise! And when rain poured hard, the roof leaked. Randy put out buckets in strategic places, and food kept being served.

Other elements of the patio that are fondly remembered include the hostess stand which was called "the rhino" because it was built like a rhino—cut out of granite to accommodate a computer screen and supplies for hostesses. Dano had started creating artistic metal sculptures, and he

*Sunset Grill patio.*

*Sunset Grill's 3-year anniversary, November 1993. Have fun and find: Marilyn, Suzanne, Jerry, Randy, Robynne, Rainbow, Paul, Dale, and others from Sunset's past.*

crafted a grape vine with grape clusters and leaves for the front entry way. The problem was that one of the leaves came off inadvertently and stabbed a customer.

No matter. Friends and guests treasure many happy memories gained from gathering on the patio. I recall the time Robynne and I were working late in the office and decided we needed a break. Instead of getting our dinner to go, we walked up and got a table on the patio. When we sat down and ordered, the crowd was slow and that was good for our relaxation/break plan. Then suddenly—as it often happens—the restaurant was slammed. We had not been served our food yet, but we sat and watched the servers—our friends—rushing around (being in the weeds as it is called in restaurant slang). We decided we could rest later—we needed to help. So, we got up, bussed our table, reset it, and told the hostess to seat it. We then proceeded to get out waters and to bus other tables. I don't remember how or when we had our dinner. I only remember the comradery and the feeling of satisfaction of being part of a group of people providing service and good food to customers.

Suzanne had her wedding shower on the patio. Randy and Sonata had a dinner for family and friends the evening before their wedding on the patio. I enjoyed hosting my friends Tore Andersen and Ottar Johansen for dinner on the patio when they visited from Norway. I recall waving to friends in cars as they drove by or on the street as they headed to the restaurant. We'd pull together tables and order drinks and appetizers and enjoyed the open air, great food, fun drinks, and each other's company.

What a time we had. (Karren Pell)

## SAYING GOODBYE

I t had rained earlier in the evening. Randy and his wife, Sonata, and my husband, Tim, and I were meeting friends Suzanne and husband John, and Jerry and his wife, Mitzi. Suzanne and Jerry and Randy and I had all worked at the Sunset Grill together for many years. As Tim and I walked toward the Cabana Restaurant with Randy and Sonata, I forced myself to look at the Sunset Grill across the street with the "For Sale" sign in front. I knew our friends were waiting inside the Cabana, but my steps slowed. Hubby, Randy, and Sonata proceeded toward the door. But I had to turn away and walk in the opposite direction down the sidewalk because I felt so sad. It WAS sad–damn it! Just plain old sad. I wiped my eyes and wondered if I had ruined my make-up–after all I was in NashVegas–and composed myself. This was to be a fun evening with friends. I turned to walk back and saw Randy walking to meet me. He didn't have to say a word. We walked inside the Cabana and everyone looked at us rather quizzically. After all, they had been living with the reality of that "For Sale" sign for a full week. "We just got a little misty," Randy explained. Like all true friends, they all understood. We gathered at the bar and ordered wine and champagne, and somebody got whiskey. Then we went to our table and had a fine night with long-time friends. (Karren Pell)

*Sunset Grill 2014 holiday portrait.*

# CHRIS CLIMER

## "LIFE THROWS YOU PEOPLE IN YOUR WAY TO HELP YOU ALONG."

When asked to recount some of his memorable moments about the Sunset Grill, graphic designer and website and email blaster in chief for the Sunset Grill, and Midtown Cafe Chris Climer takes a deep breath and sighed, "ooooh Mr. Rayburn!" Chris started designing ads and promotions for the Sunset Grill in the late 1990s while working for David McKenzie at McKenzie Advertising. He has witnessed the closing of the Sunset Grill and the selling of Cabana and feels like he has been through "thick and thin" with owner Randy Rayburn's restaurant enterprises.

While Chris explains that his work was mainly "behind the scenes with the Sunset Grill, he did share a fun story about a certain promotion. Chris and his staff had been working on a series of ads promoting Wagyu beef at the Sunset Grill. Chris had presented several approaches and Randy had sent every one of them back. Chris admits he was burning the midnight oil and his copy writer was banging his head on the desk trying to figure out, "What does this guy want?" Out of sheer frustration he had an out-of-the-box idea. He created a large ad that was headed with large bold letters: "Sexy Beef." The ad then included some info about the Sunset Grill Wagyu beef promotion. To his amazement, Randy said "Run it." Indeed, it ran for several weeks. Chris said that sometimes he'd just end up scratching his head but that ultimately working with Randy on Sunset Grill promotions "helped me develop a tough skin."

Looking back, Chris muses that "Life throws you people to help you along," and that these days "its good to just go by Midtown Cafe and talk with Randy and get his perspective on things." (Karren Pell)

## CHRIS'S MIDTOWN CAFE FAVES

**VOODOO PASTA**
**FROM SUNSET GRILL**
Grilled chicken, Bay Shrimp, Andouille Sausage in Spicy Black Magic Tomato Sauce with Fresh Egg Fettuccine Pasta

**LEMON ARTICHOKE SOUP**
Known as a classic at Midtown

*The Midtown Cafe bar where Chris gets Randy's perspective on things.*

# CRAIG CLIFFT

## "THE SUNSET GRILL WAS <u>THE</u> ONLY PLACE."

Randy Rayburn remembers that Craig Clifft was nineteen-years-old when they met at F. Scott's restaurant in 1987. Craig was attending Middle Tennessee State University getting a graduate degree in—check it out—Aero-Space Engineering. At F. Scott's, Craig had worked himself up from bus boy to general manager. Randy left in 1989 after a legal fight with the owners that Randy later won. Having an eye for restaurant talent, when Randy left, he told Craig that if he was ever looking for a job, to give him a call. Craig went on vacation and returned to new owners and new management. Randy later said he saw "the writing on the wall" and explained that "when new people come in, they want to bring their own staff. I surmised that would be case at F. Scott's, so I wanted the opportunity to have Craig work at Sunset." Craig called Randy and asked if he could "play his card." Randy said, "come on," and so began what is currently a thirty-five-year-old business and personal friendship.

Randy hired Craig as management staff but did not tell the other members of the Sunset management team. Instead, Craig trained as a server in order to learn the Sunset way (and Randy Rayburn's my-way or- the- highway way); the other staff at that time did not know he was soon to be their supervisor.

*L-R Chef Brian Uhl, Randy Rayburn, Craig Clifft at the Dirrona Awards NYC 2001*

Craig has great memories of the Sunset Grill days: "The Sunset Grill was THE ONLY place. All the beautiful people came to the Sunset Grill. And God, I remember seeing some of the most gorgeous women walk through the door. . ." Craig remembers how busy the restaurant could be: "I recall one Valentines we sold 840 covers."

Craig also has fond memories of the staff: "Everybody worked hard. I recall a host/server named Toy Van Atta liked to hug the girls who called him 'the Troy Boy.'" Craig recalls the wild staff parties and worrying about policies regarding staff drinking as being a little "loose." But all in all, he recalls the Sunset staff as "a big, dysfunctional family," that made the grill "A happy place."

In addition to the Sunset Grill, Craig was instrumental in the opening of Midtown Cafe and Cabana. Craig served as managing partner of Cabana for the entire fifteen years that he, Brian Uhl, and Randy owned it. Cabana was sold in 2020 due to issues related to the impact of Covid. As it happened, Randy was working as a consultant in

*Cabana was opened in October 2005 by Craig, Chef Brian, and Randy across the street from Sunset Grill.*

the designing and opening of the new Elliston Place Soda Shop—which is also a restaurant featuring southern food (and famous for fried chicken and meringue pies) and founded in 1939. He told the owner, Tony Giarratana, that Craig was the only person to take over as general manager and that "Craig was the smarter, better version of myself, although I was more handsome." Therefore, currently, Craig is the general manager of the historic and popular Elliston Place Soda Shop.

Four restaurants, thirty-five years, countless late nights, good times and lean times, Craig and Randy have kept their businesses and their friendship rockin.' Although Craig is not a floor manager at Midtown Cafe, he is involved as the business manager and remains an integral part of the team. Every day he helps makes new memories and new adventures while holding fast to those Sunset Grill memories: "It was a whirlwind!" (Karren Pell)

# DANO GOOSETREE

## "HERE'S TO US AND FUCK THE REST!"

I met Dano when I walked into the Third Coast looking for Randy. He was also a Tavern on the Row refugee. Although my hours at Tavern on the Row were daytime, I was often in the bar/restaurant at night hanging out and trying my best to be cool. It is not easy to be cool. One night Tanya Tucker came in with a loud entourage. She hollered at Dano "turn the lights on Dano, I'm gonna strip and show off my new store bought tits." Dano threw them all out. On her way out the door she told Randy, "Fuck you" and he relied, "Everybody else did." Always quick with a comeback that Randy.

I'll digress briefly here to share a "star" memory connected to Tavern on the Row. I was working in my office space and my boss's mother showed up and said, "Karren, come down stairs. There is someone I want you to meet." The stairway was open to the dining area, and as I walked down, I recognized Dolly Parton sitting at a table. Maybe it was the sun through the large windows, or maybe I was truly starstruck, but she shined. I was taken right over to Dolly and introduced to her. I was somewhat mortified as Dolly was obviously just having lunch, and I was embarrassed to bother her. After introducing me, she did apologize for interrupting Dolly's lunch and thanked her for coming to their restaurant. She finished by saying, "Dolly, I just feel you are part of our family." And Dolly, as regal and generous as any queen, replied, "well, that's because I am."

Back to Dano. He helped Randy close down Close Quarters (a restaurant inside the former Rock n' Roll Hotel) and open up Third Coast (aka Rock n' Roll Hotel) where he worked as the bartender-manager. He then was on the design team for the Sunset Grill bar and then worked as bartender there. Later he was a partner in opening South Street Bar and the Boundr'y restaurant near Music Row.

Randy and Dano liked to tell a tale about a regular guest (who of course was also a songwriter) who used to complain constantly about Nashville and compare it unfavorably

*Randy (in Sunset Grill shirt) and Dano at Sunset Grill's bar.*

to Los Angeles. He would say, "In LA we did it THIS way, or in LA things worked THIS way." Finally one evening Randy and Dano had enough. They bought him a one-way ticket back to Los Angeles and later that week put him on the bus! After all, like Harlan Howard used to say, "Nobody sent for you."

Dano retired from the bar tending life and became a metal sculpturing artist. He created a grape vine metal sculpture for the corner of the outside patio of Sunset Grill. He lived on family land in Lebanon, TN.

We lost Dano on March 13, 2013. We miss you Dano, and we continue to raise our glasses to your favorite toast: "Here's to us and fuck the rest!" (Karren Pell)

# (DESE) DESERIEE DAWN HAYES

I was preparing for my time of wandering in the desert (seemed like a good idea at the time and besides it worked for Moses) when I met Dese, Deseriee Dawn Hayes, in the bar of the Sunset Grill. She told me she was a singer-songwriter new to town. I offered my condolences. I told her I was also one of those creatures, but I was tired of it all and was moving to Arizona with my boyfriend. She wisely suggested I map out a Plan B—and gave me the name, address, and telephone number of her good friend who had recently moved to Prescott, AZ. I have always believed she saved my life. But that's another story for another time.

Like many other singers and writers, Dese worked as a server and hostess in addition to working on her music. Randy Rayburn has a long and established history of supporting the arts in a variety of ways—none any more important than providing aspiring country music hopefuls with what they hope is temporary employment. In addition to keeping a roof over one's head, working in a happenin' restaurant is a great way to meet people and make important contacts. At least one time, the Sunset Grill was also a place where, perhaps, Dese met "angels unawares."

Dese's story takes place when she was new to Music City. The name of the star game is to work the least amount of hours possible so as to have time to chase that dream. Like

*Above left to right: Tore Anderson, Karren Pell, and Dese.*

most singers, Dese was making contacts, recording songs, living on a shoestring, and, like some, working at the Sunset Grill. Then, one rainy morning, Dese received a telephone call from her family in Virginia with the news that her grandmother was seriously ill, and that Dese needed to come home. Now, when you are chasing a dream and scrambling to keep a roof over your head, a 500 mile trip is a daunting challenge. In fact, Dese simply did not have the money to get back home and had no idea how she would come up the money. As she sat in her apartment looking at the rain, and stewing over the bad news, the phone rang again. One of servers was calling to ask her to work for him. The Sunset Grill's patio is famously popular and everyone loves to sit on the patio. However, that day was rainy, and so the scheduled servers knew they would not make much money. One of them decided he would rather have the time off and asked Dese to work for him. Dese agreed to cover his shift even though she was pretty sure her intake would be sad. Sure enough, the lunch crowd was smaller, but Dese was happy to get any extra money. Then, just as lunch was about over, a group of twelve men came in. The other servers groaned as they were ready to leave, but Dese told Marilyn, the manager, to seat them in her section. Dese remembers that they were a fun group of men, and she joked and laughed with them and made sure they got their food hot and their drinks cold. By the time they finished, the dining room was empty, and she was the only server still cleaning her section. Then Marilyn called to her. Dese wondered if she had added something incorrectly or entered something wrong, but there was nothing bad–there was something really good. The men had left her a $1500 tip–the amount she needed to

## DESE"S MIDTOWN CAFE FAVES

**SUNSET CAESAR SALAD**
Romaine Lettuce, Sun-dried Tomatoes, Toasted Pine Nuts, Parmesan, and House-made Croutons

**TN RAINBOW TROUT ALMONDINE**
with Lemony Brown Butter and Crunchy Almonds Served with Rice Pilaf and French Green Beans

go to Virginia and see her grandmother and still make rent and utilities. Everyone was shocked. In fact, Suzanne and Marilyn went over to the table where a few of the party and remained and asked if they meant to leave that amount. They were adamant that they wanted Dese to have it. When Randy was told the whole story, he looked at Dese and told her to "Go," right then, that he and others would finish her side work.

Dese and I have been friends for all these years. Through moves, men, and music, we have always made time to have a glass of champagne at the Midtown Cafe and catch up. Recently she had a serious accident and was out of work while she recovered. I called our mutual friend and brother Randy Rayburn, and he was able to help her find employment and gave her a gift card for Sunset Grill that helped a lot too. Nashville is a place of realized, lost, and re-imagined dreams. While Dese and I have not (yet)made that dream come true of fame and fortune, we have found friends and family that love us in Team Sunset. Many of those folks and that love have transferred to Midtown Cafe. Maybe they are not always angels, but they are a blessing to us. (Karren Pell)

# LYNDA HERDELIN

### "I'M REALLY GLAD I WORKED THERE."
### "WE HAD SO MUCH FUN."

The Sunset Grill had been opened barely a year and a half when Lynda joined the Sunset Crew in 1992. She had graduated from University of Tennessee and saw the help wanted ad in the newspaper. Twenty years later, although she did not work the last night, New Year's Eve, she was still an integral part of the Sunset family.

Lynda remembers the popularity of the restaurant: "People would be lined up and waiting for a table until 1:30 in the morning." During regular dinner hours a certain decorum prevailed, but when "Late Night" switched in another reality took over. Linda says, "We had our own little gang who worked late nights and we knew a lot of the customers. We had so much fun. I brought costumes, and we'd dress up. I remember Wesley wearing one of my tutus one night." Dressing up reached its heights at Halloween after the dinner hour. Lynda remembers the Halloween that Dale dressed up like Randy with a pumpkin head. Lynda recalls there was a lot of hard work at times, but they still had fun. They pulled pranks on each other. For example, she collected pennies and was always looking for specific heads. Knowing this, her fellow servers would deliberately drop pennies on the floor requiring her to bend down with a tray full of food or dishes to retrieve the penny. Even during Randy's famous line-up rants, Lynda says she and the other long timer servers used to giggle (brave girl).

Other events she recalls were when Sunset helped cater private events such as songwriter Harlan Howard's birthday Bash's held in a tent behind BMI, and other private events when she and Michael Hunt would go work off site. Lynda remembers the time

*Lynda and Bill McFadden in Sunset Grill's bar area.*

that the morning staff kept coming in and finding broken windows. Randy staked it out one night and discovered the "crazy woman who carried a gun and broke windows early in the morning." Besides crazy people, she remembers the celebrities. She broke a serious Sunset taboo and asked Boy George, who was having his birthday party in the Sunset Room, to sign her Boy George dolls—even had to rush home to get them. She also had Donna Summers sign an eight track. And she recalls that singer Mark Chestnut and songwriter Bud Lee ("Friends in Low Places") partied a little too hardy and got thrown out by Rusty Dunn.

Lynda laughs now that she "never meant to wait on tables twenty-two years, but I learned so much about customer service." Lynda calls Randy "King of Customer Service," and adds that "everybody loves Randy." Currently Lynda and her husband Chad own and operate a vintage and unusual collectibles store called "Starland" on Eighth Avenue South in Nashville. She attributes part of the store's success to skills she acquired while working at the Sunset Grill: "I am very grateful to have worked there and for all I learned. And Randy is such a good person." (Karren Pell)

# MANUEL ZEITLIN

## "RANDY MAKES EVERYBODY FEEL LIKE A SPECIAL PERSON IN HIS WORLD."

**M**anuel Zeitlin talks about the interconnected and serendipitous nature of the Midtown Cafe and Sunset Grill family. For example, he met Randy at F. Scott's. Manuel was teaching a restaurant design studio course at O'More College. He brought his students a couple of times to F. Scott's where Randy was working. The student toured the restaurant and the kitchen and Randy shared his insight with them. Manuel would often socialize at Bishop's pub (later the Tin Angel) that was owned by Mitzi's father (Mitzi is Jerry Baxter's wife).

Another connection includes Paul Harmon. At F. Scott's, Randy and Manuel were both surrounded by Paul Harmon's paintings. Manuel and his wife, Janice, were good

*Above: Manuel and Janice Zeitlin*

friends with Paul Harmon. Janice had shown Paul's work at their art gallery, Zeitgeist.

So, when Randy leased the building that was the Nashville Bicycle Shop with the aim of turning it into the Sunset Grill, he contacted Manuel for architectural plans and reached out to Janice to help him obtain Paul's work for the Sunset Grill. Manuel says, that "Randy deserves a lot of credit for having the foresight to purchase an artist's work for his restaurant when most others were trying to get artwork on loan for free.

Randy always goes above and beyond when it comes to doing the right thing."

Manuel remembers that his first set of plans were not received in a particularly joyous manner, "Randy looked at them and said, 'You're fired.' So, I left, did some work, moved the bar, added a bunch of seats, and came back in about two hours. Randy looked at it, counted the tables and said, 'You're hired.'" Those who know Randy swear that he routinely breaks the law of physics regarding two objects occupying the same space and can slip in a two top almost anywhere. Manuel claims that "Because of Randy I learned a lot about restaurant design."

As the Sunset Grill was beginning its climb to being the top trendy restaurant, Manuel was making his name known in Nashville's architectural community. But both took time. Manuel remembers that there were periods when Randy bartered food for his design services—and he was happy with that arrangement. "My wife and I at that time really couldn't afford to go out a lot, so I'd bring home dinner and a bottle of wine from the Sunset Grill."

Manuel's friend and business partner, Bill Barkley, would go to the Sunset Grill at least once a week later in the workday and share an appetizer or even an entrée and a drink. If they stayed a bit late, Bill's wife would check in, and Bill would tell her, "I'm in a meeting with Manuel." Then, after eating at the Sunset, Bill would go home to a fabulous dinner his wife had prepared. Manuel laughs and describes the situation: "Bill would always suck it up and eat the dinner his wife had prepared, apologizing for being late because he was in a meeting."

Manuel remembers that the Sunset Grill was a great hangout, "I liked to come in and hang out with Randy and whomever he was taking to." There were always people in the bar. Manuel remembers seeing a lot of music business executives like Joe Galante, as well as artists and writers who could relax and socialize and knew, as is the Nashville tradition, they would not be bothered or treated differently. "The Sunset Grill was a great hang-out. You always felt welcome—didn't worry about formal dress—you knew you would be welcomed. Randy made everyone feel like a special person in his world." A lot of good times were had, but when asked about any one event Manuel quips, "If it was a big party how am I supposed to remember it?"

When Randy expanded to create the banquet area, Manuel designed the three rooms with air walls for private meetings and lunches. The dividers allowed flexibility according to the size of the party–maybe even room for another two top.

Manuel's business also expanded. He is now recognized as the first architect/developer of what is known as "The Gulch," and saving Hillsboro Village from Vanderbilt by designing an "Urban Overlay" along with Randy who got Vanderbilt and H. G. Hill to participate in the process.

During the years, Manuel noted that Randy was able to "surf the economy–ride the ups and downs–but that his employees always came first." Manuel explains he watched Randy develop an idea of managing partners–he brought Craig in and then developed Cabana that Craig managed, and

## MANUEL'S MIDTOWN CAFE FAVES

**WINE!**
Midtown's wine list is comparable to the Sunset Grill's and offers over 40 wines by the glass

**SUNSET CAESAR SALAD**
Romaine Lettuce, Sun-dried Tomatoes, Toasted Pine Nuts, Parmesan, and House-made Croutons

also took Chef Brian in as a partner. Manuel describes Randy in 1998, setting up the culinary program at Nashville State Community College (called the 'Randy Rayburn School of Culinary Arts at Nashville State Community College') as "heroic" and refers to Randy as the "Mayor of the Nashville Restaurant scene."

Manuel says Randy is like a big brother: "He has a listening ear; he has time for everybody. I can't image a more caring person. . . What a big heart." (Karren Pell)

*Sunset Grill, 1991*

# MARILYN MERDLER

## "AS THE SUNSET TURNS"

During the twenty plus years that Marilyn Merdler was bartender and bar manager of the Sunset Grill, she watched her Sunset family go through girlfriends, boyfriends, husbands, and wives, and developed a well-known adage for these life adventures: "As the Sunset Turns." Through it all, Marilyn has been like the big sister who can be depended upon to stay calm. Well, somebody has to.

Marilyn was an icon to daytime Nashville dining. She was songwriter Harlan Howard's favorite bartender. Harland, known for standards like "I Fall to Pieces" and new hits like "Blame It On Your Heart," only wrote in the mornings. Sometimes I'd sit with Harland and he used to say writing was like making love—he couldn't do it all day

*Left to right: Bri Minter and Marilyn Merdler*

long! A few hours in the morning and the passion was spent. Come lunch time, Harlan and his entourage headed to the Sunset Grill, and Marilyn always had his drink ready–a White Russian he called "Shaky Shakers." Harlan jokingly referred to Marilyn as the "Sexpot of the Whole Wide World." He called his drinks "health food" because of the milk, and then would quip, "Go easy on the crème, that stuff will kill ya."

During one of my gypsy stages, I'd call in from wherever-on-the-road and talk to Marilyn. She'd keep me in the loop–who was working the door, who, like me, had left for unknown spaces, whose heart was broken, who was drinking too much. I early on contributed to the validity of Marilyn's phrase "As the Sunset Turns."

Marilyn's daughter Bri Minter, worked at the Sunset Grill for eight years. But Bri is not the only example of second-generation Sunset Team. Jerry Baxter's son, Julian, worked as a bus boy for a while. When Randy's son, Duke, was just three years old, he stopped by every afternoon after pre-school to see Dad. I was there one afternoon and observed that Duke walked right in, went to the reservation desk, opened the drawer, and got out his crayons, put

## HARLAN HOWARD'S SHAKEY SHAKEY

**Crushed ice**

**A shot of vodka**

**Half shot of Kahlua**

**Quarter shot of Bailey's**

Shake! Shake! Shake!
Pour into a chilled glass letting a few piece of crushed ice go into glass.

them on the table of his choice, and then walked to the dining room to say "hi" to Marilyn. Marilyn laughed, "He walks around here like he owns the place."

But Duke, even at his young age, understood, like I did, that while restaurant life whirled and banged, there was always a need for a calm and steady hand. Like the rest of the Sunset family, Duke knew that Marilyn was close by "As the Sunset Turns." (Karren Pell)

*Duke and Randy working on the patio, 2012.*

# MICHAEL HUNT

## "WAITING ON PEOPLE IS MY PASSION"

Michael moved to Nashville from Chicago where he worked for the well-known restaurant group "Lettuce Entertain You." He was handing out his resume to restaurants in Hillsboro Village and stopped at the Sunset Grill. The hostess, Christine, told him there were no current openings, but he asked if he could leave his resume anyway. It was after lunch rush—a good time to drop off a resume—and he recalls that Event Director Suzanne Coleman was sitting at table 41 eating lunch. He saw Christine give Suzanne his resume and, "I had my hand on the door getting ready to leave when Suzanne came out and said 'Come back!' She took me over to Randy, who was sitting at his booth (56) in the bar. Randy looked at the resume and said, 'We'll make a place for you.'" Michael says that place lasted twenty-one years—he counts the Megan Berry political fundraiser given after the official closing on New Year's Eve 2014, as a whole year! Michael worked the last night the Sunset was open-New Year's Eve 2014. He remembers the restaurant was really busy. He worked back in Sunset West—the back rooms were not reserved for private parties on holidays. He had no idea that was the Sunset's last night. When he got up New Year's Day, Randy had sent everyone a text with the news.

Michael has fond memories of the Sunset Grill nights, where he served as Senior Captain for all twenty-four years. On Halloween, all the servers dressed in costumes. He recalls he was shift leader, and he was fussing at the staff about their side work not getting done because they were all dressing up in costumes. Michael continues, "then Randy disappeared. In a little while he returned dressed as Julia Child. He went from table to table, all full of customers, including the CEO of Opryland, greeting them in his Julia Child imitation." Other memories involve the late nights. The restaurant stayed open until 1:30, and customers often stayed another hour. Bartender John Ray used to turn on the lights to nudge customers out. Before the software that made server check out work fast and easy, Michael remembers that many a Saturday night he and his fellow servers would work until daybreak getting side work and check outs finished. He also remembers working with Suzanne to build the banquet department. At one time the rooms, Sunset West, held regular large banquets—up to 90 people—for pharmaceutical companies; then federal regulations eliminated those events. Even so, the banquet facilities remained popular.

Michael has memories about celebrity guests too. The night Boy George came in, server Lynda Herdelin ran home and got her Boy George dolls for him to autograph. Michael recalls that John Siegenthaler

## MICHAEL'S MIDTOWN CAFE FAVES

**VOODOO PASTA**
Grilled Chicken, Bay Shrimp, and Andouille sausage in Spicy Black Magic tomato sauce with fresh egg fettuccine pasta

would "hold court" at table #74 on the patio. He remembers songwriter Harlan Howard also holding court at bar booth #56. Other personalities he waited on at the Sunset Grill included Eva Marie Saint, Annie Lennox, Faith Hill, Fred Thompson, and Trisha Yearwood.

Michael's favorite dishes at the Sunset Grill included the Chicken Blush, the Chocolate Bomb, and the Stir-Fry. He liked explaining to customer the "healthy options" on the menu.

Many of the people he worked with at Sunset are scattered to parts unknown; others work at Midtown. Michael did not transfer over to Midtown Cafe after the Sunset closed. He followed Sunset Chef Chris Cunningham to the "Gourmet Burger Flip." That did not work out as Michael had hoped. He has been at the Marsh House in the Thompson Hotel in the "Gulch" area for the last five years: "When I love a place I stay." The part he likes most about being a server is interacting with people. These days he says he likes spending time with his customers. Every now and then, he says, someone will ask, "Did you work at the Sunset Grill?" and Michael says he is glad he can smile and say yes. Michael muses that the location where the Sunset bar stood, is now a small restaurant called "Biscuit Love," and the Sunset dining rooms are occupied by the "Grilled Cheeserie" and "Za Pizza," but the memories remain. (Karren Pell)

Photo Credit: Danielle Atkins

# PAUL HARMON

## "I WANTED TO PAINT THE WORLD."

When Paul began painting as a young artist, he noticed that a lot of painters became known for painting certain objects. But Paul didn't want to work within that limitation: "I wanted to draw a wide variety of works; I wanted to paint the world." Paul's world met Randy Rayburn's world when Randy was at F. Scott's restaurant. Paul's paintings were featured there—the restaurant had them on a lease-purchase arrangement. The details were that the F. Scott's owners paid a monthly sum; as time went on, they were able to own some of the paintings. When the restaurant closed, they were able to sell the paintings—Paul says the arrangement worked out well for everyone. In addition, Randy's connection with Paul's work was an important part of Randy's plans for his "dream grill," the Sunset Grill. Currently, Randy owns the largest collection of Paul's art; many are on Midtown Cafe's walls.

When Randy was in the planning stages for the Sunset Grill, he was working on design ideas with Manuel Zeitlin. Both knew they wanted Paul's work in the Sunset Grill, so Randy called Paul, told him he wanted Paul's painting in the new restaurant, and invited him to come look at the space and get ideas. Paul recalls that he told Randy that wanting original art is a good idea, but that Randy had the plan backwards. Paul continued that "most restaurants start out thinking they want original art. But then the contractors are late, the estimated prices will run over, there will be trouble with subcontractors, and you will be tired and overwhelmed with the whole process." At that point, Paul predicted–most restaurants end up using Monet posters. But the Sunset Grill wasn't most restaurants. Nonetheless-Paul was right- time crunched uncomfortably, and costs went up and over, but no compromises were made regarding Paul's art in the Sunset Grill. Although unusual to have the art "set in stone" from the beginning, Paul said that in the planning for the Sunset Grill, the elements listed on the budget and loan were space/equipment/art.

Later, still in the planning stage, Randy called Paul one afternoon and said he had a problem and needed to come visit. Randy arrived at Paul's studio with a stack of 30 small design boards with logos for the restaurant–he didn't like any of them. Randy asked Paul to design the logo. Paul wasn't real keen on the idea. "First, I told him pointing to the stack of boards, its obvious you are difficult to please." Quick guy. "Second, I don't really do logos." Smart guy. Nonetheless, Randy persuaded Paul to "give it a shot." Paul explains that he had worked with Milton Glaser out of New York City. In Mexico, Glaser saw some primitive signage that inspired him to create a stencil typeface. Paul designed a stencil type face influenced from the Glaser stencil. As Paul tells it, "So I worked on spacing and put an oval around it, so it looked like a logo and emailed it to Randy. I didn't hear anything. Finally, I called him, and he said it was great. Said he had already sent it to the printer for letterhead, menus, and cards. Said he loved it." So that's the story of the well-known Sunset Grill logo.

As time went on, Paul's painting, *Walking Man*, became an iconic image connected to the Sunset Grill. Paul created a series of that image, all slightly different. Randy bought the first one; Her Serene Highness Princess Caroline of Monaco bought the second one. The painting was on exhibit in Monaco and was awarded the prizes the Prix de la Ville de Monaco and Prix de la Société' E.J.A. at the XXIV Prix International D'Art Contemporain de Monte-Carlo. Paul discusses the popular image: "I wanted my work to be universal. The idea of man walking from one place to see what's on the other side of the blue mountain–the horizon."

So, when Randy bought the building area in 1994 and expanded the Sunset Grill for banquet and private dining, he asked Paul to create the artwork for the space. Paul said he'd better come look at the space, but Randy said, "No, I trust you." Paul had created two large (3ft x 6ft) watercolors–a pair of waterfalls. Paul called Randy and suggested he come look at the paintings. Paul explained they were large and since they were watercolors they needed to be framed. He advised Randy that before investing that much money in them, that he might want to come see them. Randy's comment? "Nope, I'll see them when they arrive to be hung." Paul quips that he appreciated being given "enough rope to hang myself." And then more seriously adds, "When someone trusts you that much, you work that much harder to please them, and Randy gave me free reign."

Time went on and Randy came up with the idea of Paul designing a set of dinner plates. Paul felt like the plate needed to be blank—to be clean—so the food could be featured. So, he designed an image of a "saucy" young woman on the lip of the plate—but the fun part of the design required the plate to be turned over! On the backside of the plate—in French—was reproduced a signed, handwritten letter by Van Gogh to his brother, Theo: "One of these days, if all goes well, I would love to have an exhibit of my own at a café somewhere." Paul felt like that letter showed people that "art and restaurants were a pair." Paul continued that the quote showed, "I was falling in with the tradition of exhibiting in restaurants with some pretty good artists, and I'm proud to have my work hanging on the wall of a restaurant such as the Sunset Grill."

One of Paul's fun memories involving his art and the Sunset Grill involve the restroom doors. Randy called Paul and said, "I need you to do four or five doors—the entrances to men and ladies' rooms and two stalls." Paul describes a large truck pulling up and delivering all the doors for him to work on. After the work was finished, Paul mused that one of Rembrandt's most famous pieces was from "real life" —a commission for a group portrait of a company of civic guardsmen. The painting became famously known as *The Night Watch*. Paul quips that Rembrandt was hired in his age to paint civic guardsmen in *The Night Watch* and in Paul's own age he was commissioned to paint toilet doors. But it's all in fun. Paul notes that Randy "is a dream to work with and is so considerate with people he works with."

For eleven years, from 1986 to early 1998, Paul divided his time between permanent studio/residences in Paris, France and Brentwood, Tennessee. When he returned to Tennessee, he was often asked what he missed most about Paris—the cafes, the friends, the coffee? Paul explains that from day-to-day he was keenly aware of just being in Paris—the essence of Paris. "At times," he explains, "Paris washes over you, and then yes, you notice the light, the architecture, the coffee, the friends ...but it's that over all feeling that washes over you...and that's the way you should look at art."

The men walking, the waterfalls splashing, the lady smiling, the quote inspiring—they all wash over us and call to memory those days at the Sunset Grill and beckon us to continue the story at Midtown Cafe. (Karren Pell)

# POMPIE HORNER

## "EVERY DAY LIKE PREPARING FOR WAR."

Pompie started working at the Sunset Grill in 1995 and stayed until the last night—sixteen years. He has a great sense of humor and that may be what got him through all those intense Sunset Grill nights back in the kitchen.

Pompie heard about Randy and the restaurant from a neighbor who was a dishwasher. Pompie worked as a dishwasher for five years, then moved to the pantry doing salads and desserts, and then worked his way up to being a prep cook. He worked mainly on the "hot line," gaining all his knowledge on the job. Pompie credits Chef Brian with much of his training: "Brian (chef) could be mean and grumpy, but he was a great guy. I loved him. He taught me a lot—best teacher I ever had."

Looking back on working thirty-six hours a week for 19 years, some memories came to mind. Asked why did he think he stayed, he laughs and claims, "I'm crazy." But then he adds that he would get a "Feeling of accomplishment at how much you are putting out and that Randy is a great person to work for."

Pompie remembers Chefs Will Greenwood, James Reeser and "Rainbow" McClendon. He recalls "Little Non," (what everybody called the small non-smoking room before Randy, in a rather revolutionary move, made the entire restaurant non-smoking),an hour long power outage that meant no exhaust and caused the kitchen temperature to be above 120 degrees, and nights on end of "organized chaos." He remembers that 7 to 10 big parties a night was not unusual, and that Chef Brian could "put those banquets out." Noting that the turnover was unreal, Pompie recalls that "Randy would always help out until things stabilized." Nonetheless, he laughs that during Sunset's height of popularity, "everyday was like a prep for war." Then, he jokes again, "there were always the staff Christmas parties and Christmas bonus to look forward to."

Bottom line for 19 years in the Sunset Grill kitchen? "Fun times and lots of pressure." (Karren Pell)

*Randy and Rainbow in Sunset Grill's kitchen.*

# RICK SANJEK

## "YOU GOTTA HAVE CHARACTERS TO PROVIDE ENTERTAINMENT"

Rick Sanjek met Randy Rayburn at "a bar" and Randy invited him to a party that weekend. The party was a big success. Randy was renting a townhouse at the time, and it was full to bursting with the (legend has it) over 100 people who showed up. Although a great time was had by all, the ruckus proved too much for Randy's landlord, and he kicked Randy out. (Rick currently quips— "Can you imagine—Randy too loud?")

That next Sunday morning, Rick saw Randy at the bar at TGI Fridays. TGI Fridays was a hopping place in the 1970s. Randy worked as a DJ on Thursday nights and Kathy Mattea waited tables. The Hee Haw cast used to come in for Sunday brunch after filming Saturday

*Above: Rick Sanjek, Ray Harris, a big bottle of wine, and Randy Rayburn*

night. Rick complimented Randy on the party and asked what he was doing; Randy answered "scotch." Those were the days, my friend. Rick pointed to the newspaper Randy was flipping through and asked again "what are you doing?" Randy then explained he had been kicked out of his apartment and was looking for a place to live. Rick owned a house and his friend, Tim Wipperman, had just moved out so Rick offered the apartment to Randy. And so, the adventure began.

At that time, Rick had moved from New York and was running Atlantic Records in Nashville. In New York, he enjoyed a variety of places where he liked to hang out that met his criteria of good food and good wine. He needed a similar group of hip places in Nashville, and TGI Fridays was one of them. As A&R with Atlantic records, Rick was in the thick of what became known as "The Outlaw" movement with Wayland and Willie and the boys. During that time the "rock block" as Elliston Place was called, was hopping and the famous Exit Inn and Gold Rush was filled with music and fans. Rick said he grew a beard and wore a leather jacket so he could look like a celebrity too.

The boys liked to party. On one infamous Labor Day gathering, a barbecue pit party attracted over 1,000 people. Rumors remain that in addition to enough alcohol to float a battleship, over 100 hits of acid took the party to, well, the next level.

Times changed. Waylon and Willie and the boys moved to Luckenbach, Texas, and Rick moved to New York City to work at BMI as director/writer/publisher relations under Frances Preston once again. During some of this time Randy was working as a law clerk and even as an aide to political candidates. Then, Rick moved back to Nashville.

Rick had a friend who wanted him to manage his restaurant, the Restaurant de la Renaissance. Rick told his friend he didn't know anything about managing a restaurant. His friend told him that he had been in enough restaurants to figure it out. He maintained some servers were stealing from him and needed Rick working out front. Rick agreed. The next time Rick saw Randy he was looking for a job! Rick said he needed a bus boy, and Randy said he'd take it! Rick asked if he had a tux and Randy said he had two! So that got Randy hooked on the restaurant business.

Jobs changed, but the parties had continued. Randy's house, known as Squirrel Hill that he bought in 1978, became the place. Rick and Randy even created a club—the Young Trashvillians. Inspired from a quote by artist/writer Ed Bruce (who wrote "Mama, Don't Let Your Babies Grow Up to be Cowboys"), "There ain't no lower class than Tennessee Trash," $10 got the new member a t-shirt and invited to all the parties. That would be all THE parties—with the best food, prettiest girls, and all the cool people.

Randy worked for several restaurants, learning the ropes, attracting clientele and developing recipes. At one point he even attended classes at the Culinary Institute of America in New York during which time he stayed with Rick's parents on weekends. Rick says, "Randy became a restaurant personality—he developed his clientele and learned what he was doing." Finally, Randy decided to open his own restaurant. He sold his house and raised half the money; Rick stepped up and said, "I'll be your partner." Rick now explains, "I knew he had built a list of customers and developed dishes at the places he had worked. Therefore, he already had the clientele and a menu. He was knowledgeable about wine. I bet on him—put my money up." As it turned out, the Sunset Grill became the first restaurant in Nashville with an extensive list of wine by the glass.

We all know the next chapter. Rick recalls, "'the boys' (Rick, Randy & Company) used to hang out in the back corner booth of the bar." Rick had some great celebrity stories. He said once Kenny Chesney walked up to Randy saying, "Hey, do you remember me?" Randy recognized him, but as far as a personal memory, he was at an embarrassing loss. Randy stammered a bit and then Kenny said, "You gotta remember me—I used to park cars for you at Sunset Grill when you opened." Another good story featured Charlton Heston and songwriter Larry Henley. In Nashville, most songwriters really like to be recognized and often expect people to know their successful songs. One evening actor Charlton Heston was participating in a political fundraiser event in one of the back banquet rooms. Larry Henley told Rick he was a big fan and wondered if there was any way he could meet Charlton Heston. Rick, (he says Heston liked to be called "Chuck") walked through the kitchen to the back door of the banquet room and asked Chuck if it would be cool to bring Larry around to meet him. That established, Rick grabbed Larry and guided him through the kitchen

into the event. By that time of the evening and coming from the bar, Larry needed a goodly amount of guiding. Rick introduced Larry to Charlton Heston and prefaced introducing Larry by saying he was the writer of "Wind Beneath My Wings," at which point Heston commented, "Oh! That's my favorite book." Before Larry had a chance to correct Chuck, Rick got him back to the bar. However, Larry was very disappointed that his idol did not know his song! Rick said Larry stayed really upset for over two days until he told Larry that he and Chuck had conspired and were just teasing him.

*Randy, Rick, David Burnett—The Pasta Brothers Forum*

Rick remembers the good times at the Sunset Grill, "All my friends came, all of Randy's friends came and it became THE Hang-Out. A lot of those faces became regulars, and some were just passing through." When asked about some of those people, Rick explains, "You gotta have characters to provide entertainment." But the most important element was the feeling at the Sunset Grill: "Everybody felt the Sunset Grill was like home away from home because of Randy. Now it's the same at Midtown." (Karren Pell)

# ROBYNNE NAPIER

## "IT WAS ONE BIG ADVENTURE."

One of the most endearing memories I have of my friend Robynne Napier is her sitting on the top step of Randy's attic stairs talking to me. At that time, the Sunset Grill office was in Randy's attic space. My father was seriously ill, I was broke, and I needed to get back to where my family lived in North Carolina. Robynne sat down, made me stop running around, and told me I was going to be alright. She was correct. Everything worked out as life often does. But her care and her calmness helped me settle down and figure out how I was going to get past the crisis.

As comptroller of the Sunset Grill, Robynne was an old hand at handling crisis. The first year of the Sunset Grill was working, sleeping, then getting up and working. Even several years later, the restaurant required a lot of leg work and phone work during lunch rush, dinner crush, and stacks of paperwork in between. Robynne remembers that "the Sunset Grill was something Nashville needed—it was everybody's place." When I wasn't running around trying to be a hit songwriter, I helped out with a bit of everything. Both Robynne and I were called upon, in addition to office work, to pitch in at any time

*Above: Rusty Dunn, Dano, and Robynne*

running off menus, helping out as hostesses, bussing tables, and backing up servers by delivering drinks and filling waters. As Robynne recalls, "It was one big adventure."

On one of the more memorable office moments, I was working at my desk and heard the front door open. That was unusual as it was lunch rush time and everybody, but Robynne and I, were supposed to be down at the restaurant. I looked up and to my surprise and shock beheld a huge African American man looming over me. He had to be well over six feet tall. He was tremendous in size—like a football player. But that was not the element that stood out. The defining elements of his appearance was that he wore a white medical jacket, and a pair of shiny silver handcuffs dangled from one of his wrists. "I need to use the phone," he said. I was in such a panic that I just sat there, but Robynne had entered the front room from her office when she heard the door open. She was quicker than I was. She picked up the rather large phone from my desk and handed it to him. No questions asked. While he focused on dialing the phone, we slipped out the door and high tailed it down to the restaurant. We assumed we would find some level of safety down there with Randy and Jerry and the entire staff working not to mention a restaurant full of lunch patrons. But to our added surprise it seemed the source of our visitor's need for a phone was in the Sunset Grill: a prisoner on leave to receive care for mental issues had escaped en route from Vanderbilt Hospital. Our visitor in the office was the prisoner's guard—the prisoner was somewhere in the Sunset Grill! We later learned through newspaper reports that after using the bathroom , he strolled through the dining area in his orange jumpsuit and walked out the front door. He was later apprehended close to the Sunset Grill office.

Robynne and I also shared some spooky experiences at Rick Sanjek's house & office. When Rick would travel, he asked Robynne and I to get his mail. One time he asked me to house sit. I woke up in the night in an upstairs bedroom hearing movement downstairs. Then I heard steps on the stairs. I was terrified. I literally hid in a closet until daylight. Then I carefully went downstairs. Nothing was disturbed—but me. I went over to the Sunset Grill office and told Robynne about my experience. "That hateful female ghost!" she exclaimed. Well, I had to go back that afternoon and get the mail. I was so spooked I asked Robynne to go with me. The second we opened the back door we could hear multiple doors closing in the house. Although we hoped it was a ghost, we decided not to take a chance and called the police. They went through the house upstairs and downstairs but found nothing. Robynne and I had come into the house and put the mail on the kitchen counter. We followed the policeman outside and thanked him and apologized for the false alarm. We walked back into the house and all the mail was scattered across the kitchen floor. That did it. I went up, gathered my few things, and did not spend another night in that house. Rick, of course, thought it was all ridiculous: "I never experience anything," he claimed. Robynne replied, "that's because it's a female ghost, and she likes you—she does NOT like women in the house!"

Robynne also recalled a great Jerry Baxter story. A party of fourteen ladies from a local Christian school had lunch reservations. Robynne sat them at their reserved table. A few minutes later, Ralph Murphy (ASCAP), Bruce Hinton (MCA Records), and Tony

Brown (record producer) showed up in a celebratory mode and wanted a table for lunch and to toast to a record that had just hit number one! The gentlemen were frequent guests, and Robynne sat them at a four-top and their waiter brought and poured champagne. In just a few moments, one of the ladies approached Robynne and whispered that they needed to move. When Robynne asked what the problem was the lady leaned in and whispered that the gentlemen at the table next to them were "drinking." Robynne assured the lady that she personally knew the gentlemen and could absolutely guarantee there would be no objectionable behavior. Nonetheless, the lady continued to be distressed because the gentlemen were "drinking." It was lunch rush and there was nowhere to put fourteen guests together. Robynne apologized and the lady returned to her seat. In a few moments, Bruce Hinton (always the gentleman) approached Robynne and said he had overheard the conversation and that they were very willing to move. A four top was available on the patio and so Robynne moved them outside, thanking them for their consideration and courtesy. Jerry had quietly observed the situation. Passing Robynne, he commented, "You know, sometimes it takes a program to tell the Christians from the lions."

I recall that it was Robynne who set me on the path that I currently, and thankfully, continue to walk. I had returned from a sojourn in the desert. I was disheartened with romance, music, and really life in general. However, one of the projects I had been a part of was experiencing some success: *Fair and Tender Ladies*. Tommy Goldsmith, Tom House and I had musically adapted Lee Smith's novel, *Fair and Tender Ladies*, to music. Thanks to Nancy Anderson (another friend who has remained dear), the Alabama Shakespeare Festival had signed the songs as part of its Southern Writer's Project with the goal of creating a staged musical of the songs and novel. One day, as I was working in the office, Robynne suggested that such a literary project might make me attractive to a graduate program. So, I applied to several and was accepted and awarded a scholarship to the Auburn University at Montgomery Liberal Arts Graduate School. During my first year Robynne and Randy let me come back after my last class on Wednesday evening and work Thursday through Sunday afternoon so I could pay rent, buy food, and stuff like that. Robynne and Randy also gave me a computer, and Randy helped me get a car, and move some furniture that didn't fit in the car. They definitely were key in getting me set up to start a new life, and I like to think I made the best of it. After graduation with my master's degree I became an adjunct professor of Freshman Composition at Auburn University Montgomery. There I met my wonderful husband, Tim Henderson. *Fair and Tender Ladies* continues to be produced. The latest opens September 2022 by the Wetumpka Depot Players (Alabama). Tim and I celebrated our 23rd wedding anniversary in 2022.

Robynne married the love of her life, Corey Napier. Their three beautiful children are now grown. Robynne has a restaurant of her own, Circa, in Thompson's Station, the small town where she and Corey live—and where Corey is mayor! And so, it has all turned out that on that day on the steps Robynne was right! (Karren Pell)

# SUZANNE COLEMAN

O ne of my first memories of Suzanne is a comment I made that I regret to this day!! Suzanne's desk was, shall we say, very full of papers and restaurant trade magazines. In fact, an overflow had occurred and a stack between her desk and the wall was starting to be almost as high as the desk. One of my jobs was to keep the office looking somewhat orderly. When she came back to the office after lunch rush one afternoon, I asked her to clean up her "rat's nest." Now what prompted me to be so rude I am sure I don't know, but she was most put out with me and rightly so.

But mostly I recall that we shared a lot of girl giggles. Once I was bragging about NOT being rude to an office worker who knew how to punch all our buttons. Suzanne assured me that I had earned so many "stars in my crown," that my head twinkled. We thought that was uproariously funny.

Suzanne met Randy at one of the orphan Thanksgiving dinners at Randy's home, known affectionately as Squirrel Hill. Squirrel Hill can easily be considered the seeding site of the Sunset Grill. The parties, dinners, and friendships hosted in the large Tudor home laid the foundation for what Randy has always called his Sunset family. Suzanne Coleman met Randy because he was dating her best friend, Sarah Ford. One Thanksgiving, Randy's friends Rick Shulman and Rick Sanjek invited "the girls," Suzanne and Sarah, to Thanksgiving dinner. Suzanne remembers many orphan Thanksgivings. One was particularly memorable as someone put marijuana in the dressing! There were also Christmas dinners and other parties. Suzanne attended school at Vanderbilt, and after graduation she worked in real estate. But when Randy opened the Sunset Grill in November of 1990, she was part of the debut crew as a server. It wasn't long before she became one of the managers. As the banquet and special events manager, she developed the Sunset Grill's private event business. We were friends almost from the very start of both us working at the Sunset Grill.

Suzanne and I share many memories of the early Sunset days. One of the best things most people remember about the Sunset Grill is the covered patio. But the patio was not covered when the restaurant first opened. The patio was immensely popular as the music biz folks could be easily seen out and about. But if the heavens ordained rain there was a problem: there was no room inside to bring the guests. Suzanne remembers Randy walking around outside with his arms folded and glaring up at the sky as if he could by sheer will prevent rain from coming and causing him to shut down his patio. Randy was famous for finding places for "two tops" (small tables where guests sit on either side), but the inside of the Sunset at that time could not accommodate all the guests who would be seated on the patio. Finally, he could stand it no more and he designed a patio covering. But, oh no, it was no usual patio covering. But then, who would expect it to be? A brick wall rose from the ground to about table height. Then large windows that could be raised or lowered ran along that side of the patio. People loved to sit by the windows and call to their friends getting out of their cars or walking down the sidewalk: "Come on in—we've saved you a chair and ordered drinks!" The roof was retractable so on pleasant days guests could sit on the patio with the windows open and the roof rolled back and enjoy the blue skies of Tennessee. The motor that enable the roof to roll was a tad noisy and it was easy to image the hutch shutting on the spaceship Enterprise, but no one minded. On days those blue skies hid, the roof was closed and either air conditioning or heat made the area comfortable. Those of us who worked there knew the patio had to be hosed down and swept out every morning, but that was the consequence of all-night patio parties.

Another Sunset tradition was line-up. Servers would get a copy of the day's menu and "line-up" for the chef to go over it and for Randy to say a few words. Those few words were often about issues he was not happy about and so quickly developed in a tirade. I remember once I heard him address the male servers: "Gentlemen—and I use the term loosely." Suzanne remembers a time when a new server attended line-up, survived the ordeal, but then folded his apron and simply walked out.

In restaurants, servers and hosts/hostesses keep tract of guests and dinners by using a table graph. The tables are numbered, and the sections of the floor are labeled. So—a server might ask for water to be refilled on table 25 in the Sunset room, or table 12 in the bar area. When Sunset first opened, smoking was allowed in all areas except a small dining room we called "little non." Suzanne remembers a celebrity guest who came in and was seated at table 33-close to the kitchen. She said she did not recognize him, but then Don Henley himself ordered a drink and then asked if someone had been impersonating him? Suzanne recalls "the boys," Randy, Rick Sanjek, and Ray Harris, were partying at the back-corner booth in the bar area. She told them that Don Henley was "in the house," but "the boys" were too into their own party to care about a celebrity.

I also remember bringing a man I was dating to Nashville to meet my Sunset family. We spent the weekend in Nashville and, as we were leaving, Suzanne took me aside and whispered, "I hope it's everything you want it to be." That's the kind of beautiful friend she has always been—wanting the best for me.

I remember Suzanne's wedding shower was lunch at Sunset. Isn't it strange what you remember? I remember we had salmon and creamed spinach. I was off performing somewhere on Suzanne's wedding day. One of the many drawbacks to a music profession is that you miss a lot of the important events in the lives of people you love.

When I visit Nashville, I always have lunch with Suzanne and Jerry at Midtown. Sometimes Randy and my husband Tim Henderson join us. It's great to have a place where you can gather over good food with good friends. (Karren Pell)

*Sunset Grill's 10th anniversary. (left to right) front row: Susie, Robynne, Randy, Peter, Marilyn, Brian; second row: Craig, Suzanne, Jimmy; top: Jason*

# RANDY RAYBURN

## "THE RESTAURANT BUSINESS SEEMED LIKE FUN-AND IT WAS."

To think it all started with a little boy drying dishes with his grandmother. With that experience under his belt, in the fourth grade he secured a job working in the kitchen at the Park Avenue Elementary School in Milan, Tennessee: "I got paid a little bit of money, got my lunch free, but most importantly I got out of class." But those days were filled with a lot of hard work. Family members, including Randy as a child, grew and picked 5 acres of strawberries and worked at other chores to keep the family's twenty-seven-acre farm going: "If Aunt Mable didn't win a blue ribbon for her strawberries at the fair, there was hell to pay; trust me—there were some lean years."

*Above: Randy cutting the ribbon at the opening of the Randy Rayburn School of Culinary Arts at Nashville State Community College*

Now sixty plus years later, the accomplishments rack up: owned three restaurants, received a stack of awards, worked innumerable long days and countless late nights. He is credited with owning art in restaurants, starting legislation passed in 2008 that stopped smoking in most Tennessee restaurants (working with Governor Phil Bredeson, led by Robert Gowan), and having a culinary school named in his honor (the Randy Rayburn School of Culinary Arts) at Nashville State Community College. He initiated Southern, local, and regional food innovations, anti-gun legislation, electric car stations; he hosted or organized memorable events celebrating artists, politicians and benefiting progressive causes. His activities, besides being a full-time restaurateur and for the last fifteen years a full-time father, include involvement in the building of the Titan's Stadium, the preservation of Hillsboro Village (which earned him the title of "the godfather of Hillsboro Village"), and co-chaired Mayor Purcell's convention center task force in 2003-2005. He even participated in a Moderna trial at Vanderbilt for the Covid vaccine. Randy is committed to his community and his city.

Randy opened the Sunset Grill in 1990, took over Midtown Cafe in 1997, and opened Cabana in 2005. The past is full of restaurant memories: Tanya Tucker flashing her current boob job, feeding Neil Young's entire recording staff in a one hour slot, keeping Kiefer Sutherland fed, wined, and in good company during his Nashville stays, hosting ASCAP's Ralph Murphy at his office away from his office (the Sunset bar), providing songwriter Harlan Howard his shaky shakes (drink) after his morning writing appointments, hosting Boy George's birthday party, being a favorite lunch spot for Reba McEntire, Dolly Parton, and George Strait. Then there's providing the quiet spot for Neil Armstrong, John Siegenthaler, and Naomi Judd. And besides the known names, how many guests enjoyed wedding dinners (including Randy's own), engagement parties, gold record parties, and birthday parties. The eat-ertainment, as Randy calls it, continued at the Sunset Grill right down to the last New Year's Eve on 2014, and currently continues at the popular Midtown Cafe. During this half-century of creating restaurant reality, Randy has, as journalist Kay West stated, "fired, hired, or fed everybody in Nashville."

Randy did not follow a direct route to becoming a restaurateur as hinted at in his elementary school adventures. Randy graduated from the University of Tennessee in Knoxville where he received a B.A. in Political Science. For several semesters he attended the Nashville School of Law. Still following that path, he worked at various jobs in Democratic party politics. He helped with the Tennessee races for the gubernatorial and US Senator races, and a race for president by Senator Lloyd Benson (D-Texas). He also worked as a campaign press secretary–and hated it.

So he decided to try another reality. In 1975, he was sitting at the bar at TGI Fridays on a Sunday morning after a very large party at his place Saturday night, perusing the want ads. His friend, Rick Sanjek, saw him, came over, complemented him on the party, and asked what he was doing. When Rick learned Randy was job hunting, he invited Randy to come work as a busboy at the restaurant he was managing at the time, Restaurant De la

Renaissance. That was the second step of Randy's future. In a 2013 article in the Nashville Ledger, journalist Jennifer Justis quotes Randy's summary: "Politics and law are adversarial by nature. And yes, I'd gotten tired of the knives in my back rather than the knives in my hands. The restaurant business seemed fun. And it was."

Later on, Randy recalls that in 1978 he left his state government job to go to work for his friend and housemate, Chef Jack. D. Whatley to help open Café Ritz for Mary Douglas Holt and Chef Mary Walton Caldwell. Years later talking to journalist Chris Chamberlain for an article in StyleBlueprint, Randy reminisced that "Mary Walton taught me how to make good stocks and sauces and a better martini. She had opened the original Ritz Cafe in the summer of 1971 that introduced me to the art form prerequisites of fine dining and serving for Nashville's social and business elites. "

Whatever alchemical transformation was responsible, Randy says now that working in 1978 at Café Ritz was when he fell in love with the restaurant biz : "Working there it was about nourishing people, rather than the adversarial nature of law school and politics I had engaged in previously. The comradery of the team members during and after work was a welcome change as well."

Randy went on to work for a string of well-known restaurants including Café Ritz, TGI Fridays, Opryland Hotel, Mario's, Dunham Station, Moonbeams, Tavern on the Row, F. Scott's, Mere Bulles, and Third Coast. He helped open 14 restaurants, and worked in more. As journalist Chris Chamberlain notes: "His creation story tracks along with the growth of the fine dining in the city."

Then in 1990 Randy decided it was time to create his own restaurant: "I decided that I didn't want to turn forty and never have tried." Randy sought advice from a variety of people. His financial advisor, Gary W. Smith, told him that "if you don't believe in yourself no one else will." Then Randy sold his house and everything else he could sell to raise cash "to make my dream come true, or as I refer to it, the grill of my dreams." The Sunset Grill opened November 20, 1990. The rest is, as they say, history—a lot of people's history (and the inspiration for this book).

The Sunset Grill was THE place to be. It won awards and blazed trails. Magazine *Country America* wrote that "Patrons at this trendy spot meet to make music deals, or simply enjoy a fine meal." Roger Sovine, Vice President of BMI Nashville, was quoted as saying "some people in the music industry won't go anywhere unless they are seen. For these people, it's always the Sunset Grill." And it wasn't all about the trendy vibes. The food was fabulous. A 1994 article in *Country America* waxed poetic: "Here the food is designed to be a feast to the eyes as well as the palate."

And then it began to be, well, not as trendy. The day after the Sunset Grill closed, Jan. 1, 2015, journalist Jim Myers of *The Tennessean* summed it up: "After twenty-four years and a final New Year's Eve Throwdown, the dean of Nashville restaurateurs is turning the final key and closing the Sunset Grill." It is a place that remains in legend and memory.

These days you'll find Randy working the door at Midtown Cafe during weekdays. Weekends he spends with sons Duke, 15, and Dean, 8.

The wild, late night Sunset times are memories—for more of us than just Randy. But they are magical memories that weave strands that connect people and places. In restaurants like Midtown Cafe and Elliston Soda Shop, the magic goes on. During the Sunset years, in reference to Randy's "My way or the highway" management approach, his office staff used to refer to him laughingly (and lovingly) as "Lord Rayburn." But maybe, rather than an old-world noble, he actually is a wizard. And we all remain under his Sunset Spell.

So if you're yearning for a revisit of the enchantment—go visit Randy at Midtown Cafe. You'll find Randy smiling and standing at the front door. Behind him hangs the Paul Harmon painting, "The Man with Rainbow Eyes." Sit down and let Gina bring you a glass of champagne—or drink of your choice. Let Doug bring you a big bowl of voodoo pasta or Dale serve you a lovely lamb dinner. Ah....many of the best parts can be still be found right there! Randy is still turning out excellence: "We are only as good as the last plate we serve to the last customer."

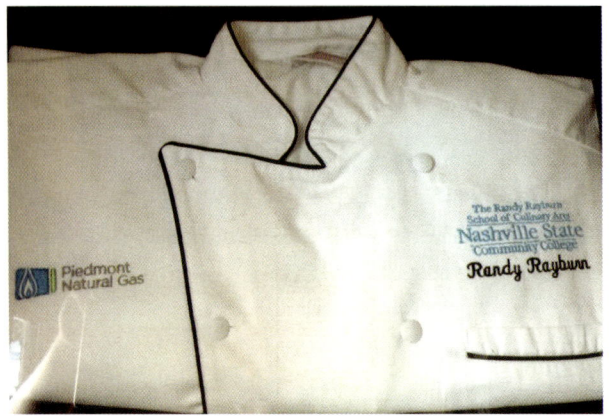

*Randy's chef jacket; students can now attend the Randy Rayburn School of Culinary Arts at Nashville State Community College.*

And Midtown Cafe offers more than just memories—check out Chef Max Paxtor's Chipotle Hummus or the tasty Shrimp and Grits. And Midtown is open for breakfast, lunch, and dinner!

Go by and enjoy being in touch with some Sunset memories, plus the excitement of trying a new dish. It's all waiting for you. (Karren Pell)

# NEVER GIVE UP

On Tuesday, March 17, 2020, I faced a startling new reality for my businesses and my two young sons (then 12 & 6), along with 50 plus employees and their families of Midtown Cafe and Cabana. Due to Covid 19, I faced the hardest business and personal decision of my lifetime impacting all of our futures.

The SEC tournament the previous Wednesday had shut down, and various states and cities were beginning to take drastic actions that month in response to Covid-19. Around 2pm, I called my operating business partner of Cabana, Craig Clifft. I told him I had decided to shut down Midtown Cafe operations indefinitely as our 33-year-old business was empty that breakfast and lunch due to the Covid pandemic panic that filled the media, online, and literally the air.

Asking him what he thought of my decision to close indefinitely, Craig replied that Cabana should close as well as he had tested positive that day. His wife, who worked at Vanderbilt Children's Hospital, had tested negative, which turned out that weekend to be a false negative.

Sharing the news of our shutdown with my daytime staff plus night shift when they arrived at work that afternoon broke my heart as it dawned on me that I had no idea of what the future would bring for all of us. How would we survive, and pay our bills, and protect our families from the challenges around all of us? As I recall the unknown confronting us then, I feel connected to the stories of the tragedy to Ukrainian families torn apart or dying as pawns in Putin's Neo-Stalinist geopolitical Soviet reborn legacy ambitions.

We began to clean up for closing down that night and asked all staff to come in early the next day to prepare the building to shut down until circumstances allowed us to reopen. All available staff came in the next day as we all prepared systems' sanitation for an indefinite shutdown. Charlie Strobel, who founded Room in the Inn (the shelter and kitchen for those in need), is a good friend; so I called Rachael Hester, the executive director. She sent a truck the next afternoon to pick up all the perishables for their campus off 8th Avenue that had not been donated to my staff.

Later that week, after cashing my employee's payroll checks for the previous week and getting all eligible for TN Unemployment, I started a GoFundMe Facebook account to help support our staff which raised over $10K from our gracious customers. Doug Stevenson handled the distribution of funds to those with families whose bills that unemployment funds were unable to cover like rent and more.

Soon afterwards, Congress passed the "Payroll Protection Plan" and even though Craig had "Long Covid," he was finally able to get our information to our CPA, Rob Taylor, who was able to finally secure an SBA-PPP funding grant that allowed us to reopen Tuesday, May 12, 2020. After taking all of the equipment out of the kitchen and deep cleaning all surfaces floor to ceiling before reopening, we reduced the menus and prepared our POS and website for TO GO and pickup service.

Several longtime employees moved away from Nashville, and some had health issues and fears of returning to work serving the public during a pandemic. Most of the kitchen crew chose to return to work while only one manager, Gina Kochevar, chose to return at that time to manage night shifts with first one, then eventually, a second server. Longtime bar manager, Patrick Petzko, suffered a mild stroke that summer and has never been able to return. On days, I reopened weekdays managing and had one server until General Manager Doug Stevenson returned in August after completing some medical treatments. Business was alternately slow and then overwhelming, but we persevered as ever so slowly Nashville and America recovered and paused from Alpha, Delta, and now Omicron with everything else along the journey.

My landlord was a magnificent partner during all this time as our first PPP grant allowed us to pay back rent through October. A new Tennessee Economic Development

Grant of $20K, then another $30K, allowed me to keep our doors open through 2020. In December of that year, we sold Cabana, which became Cabana Taps, as I would not sign a personal guarantee on its lease for the next 5 year lease option as weekly sales did not even exceed monthly rent payments. That sales income helped buy time until Congress passed the second SBA-PPP funding, which allowed me some financial breathing room in 2021.

Tony Girantana had hired my hospitality consulting firm in fall of 2019 for a project in his iconic 505 residential towers on Church Street. He then retained me personally in 2020 to put together his dream project to save the historic 1939 Elliston Place Soda Shop that he had an option to purchase. Elliston Place Soda Shop wound up going in next door to its original building and reopened last May of 2021 with Craig Clifft as General Manager. January, 2021 we decided to postpone the Soda Shop opening for the third time due to pandemic marketplace challenges. I finally returned to Midtown full time February 2021. Midtown slowly grew as we did a quarter of our annual revenues in the first half of that year and three quarters the last half finally breaking even in late summer. Then Delta rolled across our nation and we bottomed out in August / September; However, we rose to the busiest month ever in October. That rise was followed by Omicron which savaged our revenues in January, but we have been recovering since Valentine's. Over the two years almost $2M in direct business losses or valuations were gone. But, I am fortunate to be healthier than in recent years, reasonably happy with two beautiful thriving boys, and a Midtown Cafe finally returning once again to its finest hours as it was two years ago.

Last summer as business was growing, I decided to raise wages for ALL of my employees front and back of the house, to retain and attract new and subsequently returning longtime employees. That action worked as we added several longtime industry professionals to our teams, and four former employees from long before the pandemic returned to us. We now have seven more employees than pre-pandemic, and serve more customers than ever having opened for Breakfast / Brunch on Saturdays and Sundays due to the wise counsel of Gina and Doug that I fortunately acted upon. What a blessing and surprise weekend days have been! We await the return of more locals to their office workplaces near us to boost our local daytime business guests. Tourism has taken on stronger guest numbers of visits over the past two years, which is the opposite of when

*Midtown Cafe breakfast entrees*

we closed that March. Business is getting better, and I love seeing friends and their smiling faces upon returning.

During these last two years, I have found myself challenged as never before on a professional level, while being confronted initially by what I have called the Longest Spring Break in History for my young sons. Even though divorced, their mother and I worked together to protect and shield them in safety. We provided graduate students who helped during school days while we worked. Later we arranged to have tutoring for them during online school which was a difficult and challenging learning environment for both boys. Early last year they went back to Metro elementary and middle schools, but they were far behind, as were most of their peers apparently. We were able to continue their tutoring sessions, and they enrolled in the fall in their new schools in Sumner County. My biggest concerns all along had been not only for their physical health, but their mental health issues given their physical isolation from friends and media reports of emotional challenges all across our nation. Fortunately, they seem to have survived well, and their resiliency amazes me.

Both boys received vaccinations as soon as available for their age group as I decided to trust doctors and scientists given my adult lifetime of experiences with politicians' opinions on all sides of the aisle on any issue. Feeling helpless at the time, I chose to do something to try to be of service, so I participated in the Vandy Moderna trials where, through the grace of God, I received the "good juice" as Dr. Buddy Creech, head of the study shared with me January of '21 by phone. I am looking forward to meeting him in person some day and buying his meal as he said he loved Midtown and Elliston Place Soda Shop from his undergraduate era.

Today, Midtown Cafe and my work family there (with more employees than ever), along with Duke, Dean, and I offer our thanks and blessings to all who helped us along the way with support in any and all aspects of our lives. I am looking forward to the next chapters in this life's journey, even with challenges known and unknown ahead. My Milan High School mascot was a bulldog, which my closest friends call me still on occasion for good reason. In High School, I learned from the sports' fields as well as the classrooms to never give up on effort or hope.

Finally, let me offer my personal praise to the new Churchillian figure of our era for his courage and grace with which he leads his people and inspires the world in the fight for freedom against "Bad Vlad" Putin. "The question for us now is to be or not to be," Zelensky said to the British Parliament evoking Shakespeare. "I can give you a definitive answer: It's definitely to be." Again, I feel the connection to the people who are suffering in this crisis. To continue with Hamlet's musings, they, like us, took up "Arms against a sea of troubles." May they, like us, never give up and come through to a new reality. (Randy Rayburn)

# RECIPES

# FRIED GREEN TOMATOES BENEDICT
## With Poached Eggs and Chipotle Aioli

Fried Green Tomatoes—a classic Southern dish right? Hold on your Aioli—it's not that simple!

Take "tomato." Southern-right? Nope! Tomatoes originated from ancient Mexico: tomatl in Aztec language, Nahuatl. How about the fried green part? Southern-right? Nope again! Food historian Robert Moss attributes the dish to Jewish immigrants who settled in the Midwest and Northeast. According to Moss, in a 1940 edition of the Dothan Eagle (Dothan, Alabama newspaper), the editor commented that "no self-respecting Southerner would dream of eating a Fried Green Tomato." Nonetheless, after the novel by Alabama writer Fannie Flagg, and the 1991 movie "Fried Green Tomatoes" popularized the dish as a favorite of the work's "Whistle Stop Café," fried green tomatoes became a southern staple. So that takes us to "Benedict." Legend has it that a hungry wall street banker brought "Eggs Benedict" into the world. In 1894 in the Waldorf Hotel, New York City, Lemuel Benedict ordered two poached eggs on top of buttered toast, crispy bacon, plus hollandaise sauce. The chef, Oscar Tschirky loved the dish, and so there you have it. Except Midtown's dish does not feature Hollandaise sauce. Midtown's Benedict features a Chipotle Aioli. Chipotle—I bet you already know—is a Mexican pepper. Again—they are attributed to the Aztecs—the word in the native Nahuatl is "Chilpocto." They are not a specific type of pepper; they are smoked and dried jalapeno peppers. But what about aioli? Simply explained, aioli is mayonnaise with any of numerous twists. And Midtown's is wonderful. It will bring warmth to your tummy and light to your morning. So there you have it. From the Aztecs, to a southern novel, to the Waldorf Hotel, to bringing light to your morning---here it is for you at Midtown Cafe. Order this breakfast up first thing and shine all day!

## CHIPOTLE AIOLI

| 1 each | chipotles in adobo | 1/2 each | lime, juiced |
| 1 cup | mayonnaise | Pinch | salt |

Combine all ingredients in a food processor and blend until smooth. Adjust seasoning to taste.

## FRIED GREEN TOMATOES

| 2 each | green tomatoes | 1 tsp | salt |
| 1 cup | buttermilk | 1 quart | vegetable oil (or enough to fill your pan 2 inches up) |
| 1-1/2 cup | Panko breadcrumbs | | |

Slice green tomatoes into half inch slices and soak in buttermilk for 30 minutes. Season bread crumbs with salt and mix well. Pull green tomatoes out of buttermilk and press into Panko, flip and make sure it is well coated. Place oil into a deep frying pan an inch up and heat oil to 350. Place a few tomato slices in at a time, making sure not to overcrowd the pan. Cook for about 2-3 minutes and flip, each side should be golden brown. Place on plate lined with a paper towel.

## BLANCHING ASPARAGUS

8 pieces   asparagus, trimmed

While frying the green tomatoes, put a pot of water on to boil and some salt. Blanch the asparagus by placing them in the boiling water and cooking for about 2 minutes, or until the color brightens. Set aside.

## TO POACH EGGS

| 4 each | eggs | 2 Tbsp | white vinegar |

Bring a large pot of water to a boil, then reduce the heat to low. Stir the vinegar into the water and add the egg to the water and cook for 3 minutes. Remove the egg with a slotted spoon and dab it on a paper towel to remove any excess water. Serve immediately.

## ASSEMBLE INSTRUCTIONS FOR 2 PEOPLE

Place 3 fried green tomatoes on each plate, then top with 2 eggs. Put a tablespoon of chipotle aioli on each egg and top each plate with 4 pieces of asparagus. Serve and enjoy.

# NASHVILLE PIGS IN A BLANKET

**Two Biscuits with Mild BBQ Dry Rub Roasted Pork Tenderloin Served with Two Eggs Anyway and Sides of Alabama White Sauce and Country Sausage Gravy**

The biscuits are flaky and warm, the dry rub is crisp and tangy, and the eggs are like you like 'em—gotta love it. So you got the tenderloin cooked in a dry rub BBQ, but just to make sure you got enough of that BBQ flavor, this dish features a side of Alabama White Sauce. A BBQ sauce with mayonnaise as a base instead of tomatoes, Alabama White Sauce was invented in 1920 by Bob Gibson. Bob was over six foot tall and weighed in around 300 pounds. When he wasn't at work on the L&N Railroad, he was turning out pit cooked BBQ in his back yard in Decatur, Alabama. His BBQ became so popular he opened a store and along with the chicken and pork he smoked, he sold his white barbecue sauce. Midtown Cafe makes its own, and you are sure to love it. PLUS, you get Country Sausage Gravy. So much to love.

## BISCUITS

Yield: 4 large biscuits

| | | | |
|---|---|---|---|
| 1-1/2 cups | flour, plus more for work surface | 1/2 tsp | iodized salt |
| 2 tsp | baking powder | 1/4 cup | sugar |
| 1/2 Tbsp | baking soda | 4 Tbsp | butter, frozen |
| | | 2/3 cup | buttermilk |

Preheat the oven to 400 degrees. Combine flour with remaining dry ingredients and pass through a sieve to remove any clumps. Take frozen butter and grate with cheese grater into the flour mixture. Mix the butter in with your hands until well combined but do not overwork to melt the butter. Add in buttermilk and mix until mixture is moist. Flour work surface and gently spread the biscuit dough, sprinkle with flour and roll into an even 1 inch layer. Cut with a biscuit cutter and place onto a parchment lined baking sheet, keeping biscuits close together. Bake at 400 degrees for 8 minutes. Rotated pan and cook additional 8-9 minutes or until cooked through.

## RUBBED PORK TENDERLOIN

| | | | |
|---|---|---|---|
| 10oz | pork tenderloin, cut into 4-5 oz portions | 1 Tbsp | onion powder |
| 2 Tbsp | paprika | 1 Tbsp | chili powder |
| 2 Tbsp | brown sugar | 1/2 Tbsp | ground black pepper |
| 1 Tbsp | granulated garlic | 1/2 tsp | salt |
| | | 1/2 tsp | cayenne |

Mix all the dry ingredients in a bowl. Coat each piece of tenderloin in oil, then coat with mixture. Place in an airtight container and marinate for 3 hours to overnight. Once marinated, preheat the oven to 400 degrees. Place marinated tenderloins on a greased baking sheet and roast for 25-45 minutes depending on desired doneness, but at least 145 degrees internal.

## ALABAMA WHITE SAUCE

| | | | |
|---|---|---|---|
| 1 cup | mayonnaise | 1/2 tsp | ground black pepper |
| 2 Tbsp | apple cider vinegar | 1/4 tsp | garlic powder |
| 1 Tbsp | prepared horseradish | 1/4 tsp | paprika |
| 1/2 tsp | salt | 1/4 tsp | sugar |

Combine all ingredients and mix until well incorporated

## COUNTRY GRAVY

| | | | |
|---|---|---|---|
| 1 Tbsp | butter | 1/2 tsp | salt |
| 1 Tbsp | flour | 1 Tbsp | ground black pepper |
| 1 cup | milk | | |
| 4 oz | sausage, cooked and crumbled | | |

In a skillet, cook together your butter and flour for about 2 minutes until fragrant. Slowly add in the milk while constantly stirring. Add in sausage, salt, and pepper and cook until thickened, about 5 to 7 minutes.

## TO ASSEMBLE FOR 2 PEOPLE

Slice the pork tenderloin into 1/2 inch slices. Cut each biscuit in half and add about 2 oz of pork. Place 2 pork biscuits on each plate with 2 fried eggs and serve with Country Gravy and Alabama White Sauce.

# CHEF BRIAN'S FRENCH TOAST

**With Peach Compote Topped with Jack Daniel's Peach Compote and Whipped Cream**

Midtown attributes their version of French Toast to Chef Brian because the egg and milk mixture the bread is soaked in is the same as Chef Brian's famed dessert-Creme Brulee. Very fancy, and more importantly, very good. A legend persists that a man named Joseph French invented French Toast around 1724, but he left out the apostrophe after his name. However, most food historians agree that French Toast is an ancient dish that originated in Rome around the 5th century. Medieval European cooks liked the dish because the recipe allowed old bread to be used –thus the dish was called "Lost Bread."But "Lost Bread" is neither exciting or appetizing, so most food historians assume that the term "French" was assigned to it to make it sophisticated and glamorous along with very good. That brings us to Jack Daniel's part. Everyone knows Jack Daniel's Tennessee whiskey is a fine brew. There is only 1 tablespoon in this recipe, but when something as good as Jack Daniel's is used then everything else becomes very very good.

Now to the peach compote. Wikipedia notes that compotes were a popular dinner item in Medieval England due to the belief that fruit cooked in sugar syrup balanced the effects of humidity on the body. And besides that, it is very good. So, there we have it. From the ancient Romans to medieval chefs, to Tennessee whiskey makers, Midtown's French Toast pulls it all together and presents a beautiful treat that is amazing, and very very good.

## JACK DANIEL'S PEACH COMPOTE

| | | | |
|---|---|---|---|
| 1 cup | peaches, peeled and sliced (if not in season, frozen is fine) | Pinch | cinnamon |
| | | 1 Tbsp | Jack Daniel's |
| 1 Tbsp | sugar | 2 Tbsp | water |

Combine ingredients and cook over medium low heat 20-30 minutes or until it becomes a loose jammy consistency.

## FRENCH TOAST

| | | | |
|---|---|---|---|
| 5 each | egg yolks | 1 loaf | Challah bread, cut into thick slices |
| 2 cups | heavy cream | | |
| 1-2/3 cup | sugar | 4 Tbsp | butter |
| 1/2 tsp | vanilla extract | | |

In a bowl, beat yolks and sugar together until light. Stir about a quarter of the cream into this mixture, then pour sugar-egg mixture into cream and stir. Pour into a deep flat bottomed dish. Butter a skillet and bring to medium heat. Dip each slice of challah into the batter, and place in the pan. Cook 2-3 minutes on each side or until golden. Serve with peach compote or syrup.

APPETIZERS

# CHICKEN CROQUETTES
**Served with a Sweet Pea Sauce**

Croquettes are credited to France. In 1898 Monsieur Escoffier, the founder of the classical French cuisine, together with the help of Monsieur Philias Gilbert, wrote down the recipe. Lord only knows how long they had been making it. The green pea is an ancient, cultivated food. Pieces have been found dating back to the Late Neolithic period (7000-5000 BCE). Lord knows how long they had been growing them. The old adage "alike as peas in a pod" refer to the identical nature of a group of peas nestled in their pod. That characteristic inspired monk Gregor Mendel to study peas for over ten years in his monastery garden in what is now the Czech Republic. From his studies, he formed the first theories of heredity and thus earned the title "The Father of Genetics." Even though he did not discover genes. Fascinating stuff, pea sauce.

## PEA SAUCE

| | | | |
|---|---|---|---|
| 1 Tbsp | butter | 1 tsp | sugar |
| 1 Tbsp | flour | 1/4 cup | frozen peas, thawed |
| 1 cup | heavy cream | | |

In a pan, heat butter and flour to medium high heat and cook for 2 to 3 minutes until fragrant. Pour in the heavy cream, sugar, salt, and peas. Cook for 10 to 15 minutes, or until thick.

# CROQUETTES

Yield: 8 croquettes

| | | | |
|---|---|---|---|
| 1 lb | chicken breast | 1 Tbsp | chicken base |
| 1 each | carrot, peeled | 1/4 tsp | cayenne |
| 1/2 each | onion, small | 1/4 tsp | ground black pepper |
| 1 stalk | celery | 2 Tsp | mayonnaise |
| 1 each | egg | 2 cups | Panko bread crumbs |

Preheat the oven to 400 degrees. Cut the chicken breasts into quarters and place on a greased baking sheet. Roast for 15 to 20 minutes or until cooked through. Cool completely and place into a food processor. Chop until minced and place in a large bowl. Add carrots, onion and celery into the food processor and chop until well minced. Strain out the excess water and add to the chicken. Process the bread crumbs and add 1/3 to the chicken. Reserve the rest on a plate or shallow flat dish. In a small bowl whisk the egg, chicken base, cayenne, black pepper and mayonnaise. Add to the chicken mixture and mix with a wooden spoon until well combined. Portion in 2 ounce balls and press into reserved Panko. Heat a deep sided pan with approximately 2 inches of vegetable oil to about 350 degrees. Cook for 4-5 minutes and flip. Continue an additional 4-5 minutes until golden brown on the outside and internal temp of 165 degrees. Serve with Pea Sauce.

# CRISPY BRUSSELS SPROUTS

**Tossed in Honey Lime Vinaigrette with Apples, Candied Walnuts, Mandarin Oranges and Tennessee White Cheddar Cheese**

As their name infers, Brussels Sprouts originated in Brussels, Belgium. The French (of course) named them in the 18th century, and vinaigrette in the 19th century. The walnut is a tad more intriguing. According to the website, Chandlerorchards.com, the Romans called them "Juglans regia," and that is also their scientific name. That can be loosely translated as "the glands of Jupiter," and the Romans referred to them as "Jupiter's royal acorn." As might be guessed at this point, the Romans believed walnuts were an aphrodisiac. Now, go ahead and giggle, but modern doctors recommend walnuts as a food source that can improve sperm count. And to continue, in the first century Rome, it was customary for bride grooms to scatter walnuts among the young guests at a wedding while they all danced and sang bawdy songs. You gotta hand it to them–those Romans knew how to throw a party. One final note on walnuts–they were among the food found left on a table in the temple of Isis on August 24, 74 AD–the day Mount Vesuvius erupted and destroyed Pompeii. Mandarins oranges are named after high ranking officials in China who wore bright orange robes and introduced the fruit to England. So we have wandered from Belgium, Rome, France, and China, but we end back in good ole Tennessee with Tennessee White Cheddar Cheese. So let's be happy and content with enjoying the cheese because it's probably not that good an idea to go throwing your walnuts around the restaurant, dancing and singing bawdy songs. Also, its pretty safe to assume most guests are not in any danger of immediate demise by a volcano. So. Just relax and enjoy those Crispy Brussels Sprouts.

## HONEY LIME VINAIGRETTE

| | | | |
|---|---|---|---|
| 4 tsp | lime juice | 1-1/2 Tbs | Dijon mustard |
| 1/3 cup | rice wine vinegar | 4 tsp | sesame oil |
| 1/4 tsp | salt | 1 oz | roasted red pepper |
| 1/3 cup | honey | 1/2 tsp | ground black pepper |
| 1/2 each | yellow onion, julienned | 1/2 cup | olive oil blend |
| 2 Tbsp | cilantro, rough chopped | | |

Combine all ingredients except oil into a tall container and use an immersion blender puree until smooth. Slowly pour in oil while blending and adjust seasoning to taste.

## CANDIED WALNUTS

| | | | |
|---|---|---|---|
| 1 cup | walnuts | 1/2 Tbsp | water |
| 2 Tbsp | sugar | Pan spray (as needed) | |

Preheat oven to 350. In a bowl, mix walnuts with sugar and water. Line your baking sheet with parchment paper and coat with a layer of pan spray. Spread the nuts in a thin layer and bake at 350 for 5 minutes, pull out and stir. Continue cooking for an additional 4-5 minutes or until crisp.

## TO FRY BRUSSELS

| | |
|---|---|
| 8 oz | Brussels sprouts, halved |
| 1 quart | vegetable oil (or enough to fill your pan 3 inches) |

Get a deep pan and fill to 3 inches with oil and bring up to 350 over medium heat. Add in half of the Brussels sprouts and cook for about 4 minutes or until golden. Stirring occasionally. Remove with metal strainer and place on a paper towel lined plate to drain. Repeat with the second half.

## TO ASSEMBLE

| | | | | |
|---|---|---|---|---|
| 8 oz | fried Brussels sprouts | | 1/4 cup | apple, chopped |
| 1/4 cup | honey lime vinaigrette | | 1/4 cup | Mandarin orange |
| 1/4 cup | candied walnuts | | 1/4 cup | white cheddar, shredded |

Place Brussels in a bowl and add all other ingredients. Toss together and plate.

# LEMON ARTICHOKE SOUP

**Artichokes and lemons blended with a creamy chicken broth**

This famous soup was reason Midtown was listed as "One of The 17 Best Places to Eat Soup" by Eater.com. The review made it clear: "For over 30 years, people have been coming in, sitting down, and saying, 'I'll start with the lemon artichoke soup.' There's a reason for that: you don't mess with a winner, and this absolutely is. The ingredients are simple-artichokes and lemons, blended with creamy chicken broth—yet they create something that's more than the sum of its parts-a tongue-tingling wake up call to begin a meal (Ashley Brantley; Dec. 14, 2020)." Legend has it the recipe was an integral part of the negotiating process for the purchase of the restaurant. But the ingredients in the menu description is all you're gonna get. Randy says you gotta come see him to get it. Sorry. He's the boss.

# SUNSET CAESAR WITH GRILLED SALMON
## With Poached Eggs and Chipotle Aioli

Restauranteur Caesar Cardini is credited with creating the Caesar Salad. The story goes that it was July 4, and a last-minute rush found him short on supplies–so he did as any successful restaurateur does–he made a salad with what he had, and added a theatrical touch by tossing it at the table. The original did not have anchovies; the Sunset Grill's did; Midtown's does not. Maybe Randy will toss it at your table; maybe not.

Salmon has been a lovely dinner for thousands of years in both North American and Europe. In Irish mythology, the fish is associated with wisdom and knowledge. But don't worry about gaining any intense insights or directions to long lost hidden locations. As far as it goes at Midtown, the Caesar Salad with Salmon will let you know you made a wise dinner decision.

## CAESAR DRESSING
Yield: 1 Pint

| | | | |
|---|---|---|---|
| 1 Tbsp | lemon juice | 1/2 Tbsp | black pepper |
| 3/4 cup | liquid eggs | 1/2 Tbsp | lemon pepper seasoning |
| 3 Tbsp | fresh chopped garlic | 1/2 tsp | salt |
| 2 Tbsp | Worcestershire sauce | 1-1/2 cup | shredded parmesan cheese |
| 1/2 Tbsp | red wine vinegar | 1 cup | blended olive oil |

In a tall container, combine all ingredients except oil. Place an immersion blender into container and on medium speed slowly add in oil until smooth.

## TO ASSEMBLE SALAD FOR 2 PEOPLE

| | | | |
|---|---|---|---|
| 8-10 oz | chopped romaine lettuce | 2 oz | shredded parmesan cheese |
| 1/4 cup | Caesar dressing | 2 each | salmon fillets |
| 2 oz | sun dried tomatoes | | (about 5 oz each) |
| 2 oz | pine nuts | | |

Heat grill to medium high heat and make sure grill grates are hot. Season salmon fillets with salt and pepper and lightly coat with oil spray. Place the top of the fillet on the grill and cook about 4-5 minutes on each side for medium doneness. In a bowl toss romaine with Caesar dressing and transfer to 2 plates. Top each plate with sun-dried tomatoes, pine nuts, and Parmesan. Top each salad with salmon and enjoy.

# MEDITERRANEAN PASTA
## With Angel Hair, Roasted Roma Tomato, Fresh Spinach, Artichoke Hearts and Mushrooms Tossed in Basil Pesto.

Angel hair is a poetic name for a delicate long pasta that also called Capellini. But Capellini is not as, well, poetic as angel hair. Roma tomatoes are small plum like tomatoes. Like all tomatoes, they originate in Mexico with the Aztecs; the word in their native language of Nahuatl for the tomato was tomatl. The Spanish conquistadors took tomatoes back with them to Spain and from there the tomato made it to Italy where Italian chefs fell in love with the tomato. And understandably so. Spinach originates in ancient Persia, but in good ole USA we all think of the cartoon character Popeye who boasted, "I'm strong to the finich cause I eats me spinach." On to the artichoke which is a flower or a fruit, and mentioned by Homer. Mushrooms of course are a fungus. Their speedy growth has inspired phrase such as "mushrooming" or "Popping up like mushrooms." By now your appetite is probably mushrooming. But let's briefly talk about Basil and Pesto. The Egyptians used basil in mummification, but these days we prefer it in pesto. "Pesto" comes from a verb that means "to pound." And sure, enough that's what happens to the ingredients for pesto. So, many of these the ingredients for Mediterranean pasta are Mediterranean! But Mediterranean pasta can be brought right to your table here at Midtown Cafe in Nashville, Tennessee.

## PESTO

| | | | |
|---|---|---|---|
| 4 oz | basil | 1/4 cup | shredded parmesan |
| 2 Tbsp | pine nuts | 1/2 cup | olive oil |
| 2 clove | garlic | To taste | salt and pepper |

Place all ingredients except oil into the food processor. Turn on and slowly add oil until smooth. Adjust seasoning if needed

## TO MAKE THE PASTA

| | | | |
|---|---|---|---|
| 8 oz | angel hair pasta | 4 oz | artichoke hearts |
| 2 each | Roma tomatoes | 4 oz | mushrooms |
| 8 oz | fresh spinach | 1/2 cup | pesto |

In a large pot Bring salted water to a boil. Add the angel hair and cook for 5 minutes or by package directions. In a large skillet on medium high heat and add olive oil. Add the vegetable and saute for 3-4 minutes, add pesto and angel hair and cook for an additional minute. Plate and enjoy.

# VOODOO PASTA

**With Grilled Chicken, Bay Shrimp, Andouille Sausage in Spicy Black Magic Tomato Sauce with Fresh Egg Fettuccine Pasta**

Marie Laveau, dolls with pins stuck in their heads, gris-gris, black magic—the magic and mystery of that part of New Orleans—on a plate! One of the most popular dishes at the Sunset Grill is still served at Midtown Cafe. The first few bites will let you know why this dish retains decades of popularity. Smoky, a little mysterious and lot delicious—dig in!

## BLACK MAGIC TOMATO SAUCE

Yields: 1 quart

| | | | |
|---|---|---|---|
| 1/4 cup | diced green pepper | 1 Tbsp | tomato paste |
| 1/4 cup | diced onion | 2 tsp | oregano |
| 1 tsp | minced garlic | 2 Tbsp | Paul Perdome Redfish Magic |
| 2 Tbsp | olive oil | | |
| 1 each | 28 oz whole canned tomatoes | | |

In a medium saucepan, heat oil over medium heat. Add peppers and onions and cook until tender. Add garlic and cook until fragrant. Add the tomatoes and paste and bring to a boil. Reduce heat to low and add seasoning. Cook for 30-45 minutes, uncovered, stirring occasionally. Taste and adjust seasoning.

## TO MAKE VOODOO PASTA FOR 2 PEOPLE

| | | | |
|---|---|---|---|
| 8 oz | fettuccine pasta | 4 oz | Andouille sausage |
| 2 Tbsp | olive oil | 4 oz | shrimp, peeled and de-veined |
| 4 oz | chopped chicken breast | 2 cups | Black Magic Sauce |

Bring a pot of salted water to a boil for the pasta. Follow the pastas box directions for cook time. Strain and set aside. While pasta is cooking. Heat a large skillet to medium high heat and add the oil. Start by cooking the chicken and Andouille until the chicken is cooked all the way through, about 6-7 minutes. Then add the shrimp and cook for another 3 minutes. Add the sauce and pasta and cook for another minute. Split onto 2 plates and serve.

# MIDTOWN'S SHRIMP AND GRITS

## Features Blackened Shrimp Tossed with Bacon, Mushrooms, Tomatoes, and Scallions served in Stone Ground Smoked Gouda Cheese Grits

Doug Stevenson says when he has a guest from outside the South he always recommends Shrimp and Grits as a "Southern" food. Made from corn, grits are one of the first American foods—the Muscogee Indian people introduced grits to the European colonists. Any recipe book or site will agree there are many variations of shrimp and grits. Midtown blackens the shrimp. Blackening means coating the shrimp in spices that, when cooked, turn dark. It is NOT charring the shrimp. Pairing shrimp and grits, blackening shrimp, and Cajun spices all connect the dish with Louisiana and/or the "Low-Country" of Charleston, South Carolina. The Gouda cheese steps outside the American history box: it is a Dutch cheese. It is also a very old cheese—made in the 1100's and said to be one of the oldest cheeses still made today. Another thing important to note: Grits is singular in terms of English usage. No matter how you eat them. Yes, Grits is good.

## SMOKED GOUDA GRITS

| | | | |
|---|---|---|---|
| 1 cup | whole milk | 2/3 cup | white corn grits (not instant) |
| 1-1/2 cups | chicken stock | 3/4 cup | Gouda, grated |
| 1 tsp | salt | 4 Tbsp | butter, chopped |
| 1 tsp | ground black pepper | | |

In a 2-3-quart saucepan mix the milk, chicken stock, salt, and pepper. Set over medium-high heat and bring to a boil. Once boiling, whisk in grits, until there are no clumps. Lower the heat to medium-low. Cover and simmer for about 15 minutes or until grits appear soft and thick, stirring occasionally. Stir in the butter and Gouda, taste and add more seasoning if needed.

## SHRIMP SAUCE FOR 2

| | | | | |
|---|---|---|---|---|
| 1 Tbsp | olive oil | | 2 Tbsp | blackening seasoning |
| 1 tsp | garlic | | 3/4 cup | white wine |
| 12 each | large shrimp, peeled and de-veined | | 1 Tbsp | hot sauce |
| | | | 1 tsp | lemon juice |
| 1/2 cup | mushrooms, sliced | | 4 Tbsp | butter |
| 2/3 cup | cherry tomatoes, halved | | | |

In a large skillet on high heat add olive oil and garlic, and once fragrant add in the shrimp. Cook for 2 to 3 minutes. Flip and add mushrooms, tomatoes, and blackening seasoning, cook for 3 minutes and de-glaze with white wine. Reduce to half and add hot sauce and lemon juice. Turn off the heat and stir in the butter. Split onto 2 plates with a Scoop of grits. Enjoy!

# MIDTOWN MEATLOAF

**10 oz Served with Tomato Herb Gravy, Yukon Mashed Potatoes, and French Green Beans**

Although ground patties of meat with bread were among recipes in a Roman cookbook of the 4th or 5th century AD, the American meatloaf owes its invention to another invention–the meat grinder. Merchants wanting to sell housewives the new invention created new recipes for ground meat, and the great American meatloaf was invented. Its economy and comfort made it popular through the hard times of the depression and World War II. However, the Midtown meatloaf is not altogether your mother's meatloaf. The Midtown meatloaf combines the taste and comfort of past recipes with a modern delectable tomato herb gravy. The Midtown meatloaf lets you relax in nostalgia and bask in modern cool.

## MEATLOAF

| | | | |
|---|---|---|---|
| 2lb | ground beef | 1/4 cup | Heinz 57 |
| 1 each | yellow onion, chopped | 2 tsp | salt |
| 1 each | green bell pepper, chopped | 2 tsp | pepper |
| 1/4 cup | Panko breadcrumbs | | |

Preheat the oven to 375 degrees. Place all ingredients into a bowl of a stand mixer with a paddle attachment, and blend until well incorporated. Spray a 9x5 loaf pan with pan spray and press the mixture in tightly. Wrap with aluminum foil and bake for 40 minutes at 375 degrees or until internal temperature reaches 160.

## TOMATO HERB GRAVY

| | | | |
|---|---|---|---|
| 1 cup | ketchup | 1/2 tsp | salt |
| 1 tsp | dried oregano | 1/2 tsp | ground black pepper |
| 1 tsp | dried basil | Pinch | sugar |

Place all ingredients into a small sauce pot and bring up to a simmer. Remove from heat,and cover over cooked meatloaf.

## MASHED POTATOES

| | | | |
|---|---|---|---|
| 1 lb | Yukon Gold potatoes, peeled and quartered | 1/4 cup | heavy cream, room temp |
| 1 stick | butter, soft | 1 tsp | salt |

Place potatoes in a 3 quart pot and cover with cold water and a pinch of salt. Bring to a boil over high heat. Once boiling reduce heat to medium and continue boiling until fork tender, about 10 to 15 minutes. Strain and place back into the pot. Add butter and heavy cream.

## GREEN BEANS

| | | | |
|---|---|---|---|
| 8 oz | haricot verts, blanched | 2 tbsp | butter |
| 2 Tbsp | olive oil | To taste | salt and pepper |
| 1 tbsp | garlic | | |

Heat a skillet to medium heat and add olive oil. Cook garlic until fragrant, add green beans, butter, salt, and pepper. Cook for 3-4 minutes.

## TO PLATE MEATLOAF FOR 2

Place a scoop of mashed potatoes to the center of the plate Add the green beans to one side and a large slice of meatloaf topped with the tomato herb gravy. Enjoy.

# CHICKEN PUFF PASTRY
## Filled with Chicken and Mushrooms in a Rich Creamy Sauce
## Served with Asparagus and Hollandaise

Yummy ingredients in a puff pastry is a French creation known in that fair land as "Vol-Au-Vent." That fancy phrase literally translated means "flight in the wind" and describes the lightness of the pastry. If you love asparagus, you are historically in good company as it was a fave of the ancient Egyptians and Romans. In fact, Rome's first emperor, Augustus, maintained a fleet of ships to keep him in stock. And nothing goes with asparagus better than Hollandaise sauce. Regardless of "Holland" in its name the sauce is attributed to, yep you got it, the French. So what's the deal with Holland you ask. War, my friends. During the first World War it seems France's butter production ground to a less than creamy halt. But French cooks would not be denied so they imported butter from Holland and changed the name to indicated the source. And so now, no matter where that butter comes from in Hollandaise sauce—Hollandaise sauce it is! Chicken Puff Pastry is offered as a special and special it is!

| | | | |
|---|---|---|---|
| 1 sheet | frozen puff pastry | 8 oz | chicken breast, cubed |
| 1 each | egg, beaten | 1 cup | heavy cream |
| 1 each | small onion, diced | 1 Tbsp | butter |
| 4 oz | mushrooms, sliced | 1 Tbsp | flour |
| 2 Tbsp | olive oil | 1 tsp | salt |
| 1 tsp | garlic, minced | 1 tsp | pepper |

Preheat the oven 350 degrees. Pull puff pastry out of the freezer to soften. Once soft, fold it out to a flat sheet. Cut out four large circles. Take 2 of the circles and cut a smaller circle in the middle to form a ring. Brush the circle with the egg and place a ring on top to form a bowl with a lid. Brush with egg and place on a parchment lined sheet pan. Bake at 350 degrees for 7-9 minutes until fluffed and golden. Heat a skillet to medium high heat. Add the olive oil, onions, and mushrooms. Cook till onions become tender. Add garlic and cook until fragrant. Add chicken and cook for about 10 minutes, internal temperature reads 160 degrees. While the chicken is cooking, make a roux by combining butter and flour in a small skillet and cooking for 3 minutes.

Once chicken is cooked add heavy cream, roux, salt and pepper. Bring to a simmer and cook until the sauce thickens. Serve over the puff pastry.

# TENNESSEE RAINBOW TROUT
**Served with Roasted Red Potatoes,
Sautéed Spinach and Crawfish Cream Sauce**

A rainbow trout does not live somewhere over the rainbow. It is named for a distinctive red or pink line down its body. They live mostly in fresh water and are native to the Pacific Ocean but love it in Tennessee. Red (and white too) potatoes hail from Peru. And those old foodies the Spanish Conquistadors brought them to Europe, and the potato made it back across the Atlantic to America. Spinach, on the other hand, hails from ancient Persia; Popeye didn't get involved until 1929 when he proclaimed he "was strong to the 'finich' 'cus I eats me spinach." That leaves the Crawfish Cream Sauce to learn about. When thinking of crawfish, Louisiana comes to mind. But crawfish are a traveling bunch, and some cousins even live in the Pacific Northwest. Their proper name, "crayfish," derives from an Old French word, but in America they are known as "crawfish," and answer (maybe) to nicknames like "crawdad." While none of these ingredients come from over the rainbow, this dish is plenty good enough to dream about.

## ROASTED POTATOES

| | | | |
|---|---|---|---|
| 1 lb | red potatoes, peeled and cut in 1/2 inch cubes | 1 tsp | oregano |
| | | 1 tsp | thyme |
| 2 Tbsp | olive oil | 1 tsp | ground black pepper |
| 1 tsp | rosemary | 2 tsp | salt |

Preheat the oven to 375 degrees. Toss the potatoes in the oil and spices. Lay flat over a sheet pan and bake at 375 degrees for 20 minutes.

## CRAWFISH CREAM SAUCE

| | | | |
|---|---|---|---|
| 4 oz | crawfish pieces | 1/2 cup | heavy cream |
| 1 Tbsp | blackening seasoning | | |

Heat a skillet to medium heat. Add oil and crawfish. Toss in blackening seasoning and cook for 2-3 minutes. Add heavy cream and reduce by half.

## SPINACH

| | | | |
|---|---|---|---|
| 8 oz | baby spinach | 1 tsp | garlic, minced |
| 1 Tbsp | olive oil | To taste | salt and pepper |

Heat skillet to medium high heat. Add oil and garlic and heat till fragrant. Add spinach and cook until wilted. Season with salt and pepper.

## TROUT

| | | |
|---|---|---|
| 2 each | trout fillets, skin on | Cooking spray |
| To taste | salt and pepper | |

Heat your grill to medium high or reading 400. Season fillets with salt and pepper, and coat lightly with pan spray. Place the trout skin side down and cook for 3-4 minutes. Flip and cook for an additional 3-4 minutes. Remove from heat.

## DESSERTS

# HABANERO BUTTERSCOTCH BREAD PUDDING
### Topped with White Chocolate Sauce

Bread pudding originated as a 12th or 13th dessert in merry ole England invented by cooks who needed to use up leftover bread. This ingredient caused it to be known as "poor man's pudding," but there is nothing poor about this rich dish in the modern menu. Midtown's bread pudding is rich AND exciting. Yes-exciting because Midtown's bread pudding embraces a Habanero pepper. Originally from Peru, but also used in Mexico. Archaeologists have found a Habanero that is 8,500 years old. Wonder if it is still hot? Anyway—don't worry about the heat—it is

mixed in so it just gives a bit of an exciting flavor. Then the next ingredient comes to play—butterscotch. Despite its name, butterscotch is more English in origin than Scottish and is very creamy and yummy. And THEN, as if those elements were amazing enough—it is all topped by a white chocolate sauce. The invention of chocolate is credited to ancient Mexico—before the Aztecs. So—in terms of points for origin there are two for England and two for Mexico. BUT the whole point is that, regardless of history, this is right now today an amazingly delicious dessert!

## FOR BREAD PUDDING
Yield: 8x8" pan

| | | | |
|---|---|---|---|
| 8 each | whole eggs | 1 cup | whole milk |
| 1/2 cup | sugar | 2-3 dashes habanero tabasco |
| 1 bag | butterscotch chips | 1-1/2 each baguette |
| 2 cups | heavy cream | |

## WHITE CHOCOLATE SAUCE

| | | | |
|---|---|---|---|
| 1/2 cup | heavy cream | 1/2 cup | white chocolate chips |

Cut the baguette into 1/2 inch squares and place into a large container. In a saucepan heat the cream and milk almost to a boil and add the butterscotch chips and melt. In a metal bowl, whisk together the eggs and sugar, and slowly temper the cream mixture and add the habanero tabasco. Pour the mixture over the bread and soak overnight, covered. Preheat the oven to 350 degrees. Grease 8x8" baking pan and fill with pudding. Cover with aluminum foil and bake for 1 hour and 20 minute. Remove foil and bake for an additional 20 minutes until the top becomes lightly golden. While baking prepare the white chocolate sauce by heating cream to almost a boil. Remove from heat and stir in white chocolate chips until fully melted. Set aside. Let cool for about 5 minutes and cut into 4-6 portions. Serve with vanilla ice cream and white chocolate sauce.

# JACK DANIEL'S CHOCOLATE PECAN PIE

Pecan Pie is a classic southern treat. It seems that the earliest recipes for pecan pie hail from Texas after the Civil War. A pecan pie is, all by itself, a little bit of heaven. Add chocolate, and you are heading over the edge. Add Jack Daniel's and well— what's left to be said. Can you really turn this down?

| | | | |
|---|---|---|---|
| 1 each | frozen deep dish pie crust | 1/3 cup | sugar |
| 1-1/4 cup | chopped pecans | 1 tsp | vanilla extract |
| 1-14 cup | chocolate chips | 1-12 Tbsp | melted butter |
| 3 each | whole eggs | 3 Tbsp | Jack Daniel's |
| 2/3 cup | dark corn syrup | | |

Preheat the oven to 325 degrees. Pull pie crust from freezer and bring to room temp. Mix pecans and chocolate chips and fill into pie crust, Mix the remaining ingredients until smooth and pour over pecan mixture. Bake at 325 for 40-45 minutes or until no longer liquid in the middle. Let cool. Cut and serve with vanilla ice cream.

# CREME BRULEE
## With Raw Sugar Topping

Food historians are at odds regarding the origins of this yummy dessert. Even the name is a point of discussion. In 1702, it is called "burnt cream" referring to the caramelizing the sugar topping. Then, in 1879, it became "Trinity Cream" or "Cambridge Burnt Cream" when some chef got fancy and, according to the *Oxford Companion on Food,* used a branding iron to impress the Cambridge coat of arms on top of the cream. Expect no such shenanigans at Midtown. Do expect an elegant and delicious treat.

| | | | |
|---|---|---|---|
| 5 each | egg yolks | 1-2/3 cup | sugar (plus more for finishing) |
| 2 cups | heavy cream | 1/2 tsp | vanilla extract |

Preheat the oven to 325 degrees. In a saucepan, combine cream, vanilla extract and cook over low heat just until hot. In a bowl, beat yolks and sugar together until light. Stir about a quarter of the cream into this mixture, then pour sugar-egg mixture into cream and stir. Pour into four 6-ounce ramekins and place ramekins in a baking dish; fill the dish with boiling water halfway up the sides of the dishes. Bake for 30 to 40 minutes, or until centers are barely set. Cool completely. Refrigerate for several hours and up to a couple of days. When ready to serve, top each custard with about a teaspoon of sugar in a thin layer. Using a torch slowly run flame over top until the sugar starts to caramelize, tilt slowly if necessary being mindful that the top of the dish will be hot. Serve with fresh berries.

# SELECTED BIBLIOGRAPHY

## PERIODICALS

Brantley, Ashley. "17 of the Best Places to Eat Soup in Nashville." Eater.com Dec. 14, 2020.

Chamberlain, Chris. StyleBluePrint.com

*Country America*. 1994.

Justis, Jennifer. "Randy Rayburn Adapts to Competition from the Booming Middle Tennessee Restaurant Scene He Helped Create." *The Nashville Ledger*. Friday, Dec. 20, 2013. Vol. 37. No. 51.

Moore, Linda A. "Sunset Grill Between the Fern Bars and Four Stars." *The Tennessean*. May 28, 1992.

Myers, Jim. *The Tennessean*. 2015.

Ramsey, Delia Jo. "One of 20 Great Spots for a Monday Meal Out in Nashville." Eater.com. Feb. 7, 2022.

Ramsey, Delia Jo. "21 Excellent Date Night Restaurants in Nashville." Eater.com. Sept. 8, 2021.

West, Kay. "Work That Lunch." *Business Nashville*. July/August. 1999.

Wood, Nicki Pendleton. *The Nashville Ledger*. Vol. 44. No. 8. Friday, Feb. 2, 2020, https://tnledger.com/editorial/article.aspx?id:126250.

## INTERVIEWS

Chef Brian Uhl. Interview. Conducted by Karren Pell. May 2005.

Chris Climer. Interview. Conducted by Karren Pell. May 2022.

Craig Clifft. Interview. Conducted by Karren Pell. Nov. 2021.

Dale King. Interview. Conducted by Karren Pell. Nov. 2021.

Dese Hayes. Interview. Conducted by Karren Pell. Oct. 2018.

Doug Stevenson. Interview. Conducted by Karren Pell. Nov. 2021.

Gemma Freidli. Interview. Conducted by Karren Pell. Nov. 2021.

Gina Kochevar. Interview. Conducted by Karren Pell. Nov. 2021.

John Woodard. Interview. Conducted by Karren Pell. Nov. 2021.

Lynda Herdelin. Interview. Conducted by Karren Pell. Nov. 2021.

Manuel Zeitlin. Interview. Conducted by Karren Pell. Jan. 2022.

Marilyn Merdler. Interview. Conducted by Karren Pell. May 2022.

Chef Max Pastor. Interview. Conducted by Karren Pell. Jan. 2022.

Michael Hunt. Interview. Conducted by Karren Pell. Nov. 2021.

Miguel Martinez. Interview. Conducted by Karren Pell. Jan 2022.

Paul Harmon. Interview. Conducted by Karren Pell. Feb. 2022.

Pompie Horner. Interview. Conducted by Karren Pell. Feb. 2022.

Randy Rayburn. Interview. Conducted by Karren Pell. May 2022.

Rick Sanjek. Interview. Conducted by Karren Pell. Mar. 2022.

Robynne Napier. Interview. Conducted by Karren Pell. April 2022.

Suzanne Coleman. Interview. Conducted by Karren Pell. Nov. 2021.

# ABOUT THE AUTHORS

*Randy Rayburn, Dean & Duke Rayburn at front of Midtown Cafe with Paul Harmon's Rainbow Man 2022*

**RANDY RAYBURN** has been a leading force in Nashville's restaurant scene for over 50 years. His influence reaches beyond the dining room and kitchen to the arts, entertainment, politics, and the support and training of the next generation of culinary professionals (The Randy Rayburn School of Culinary Arts at Nashville State Community College). He can be currently found at the front desk at Midtown Cafe where he is the proprietor. However, with all this activity and success, his two sons, Duke and Dean, are the joy and light of his life.

*Karren sporting a Sunset Grill shirt and posing with Denmark's Little Mermaid in the early '90s!*

**KARREN PELL** is an author, a bit of a singer-songwriter, and a retired teacher. Karren taught composition and literature for twenty years. Karren has written six books-four with co-writer Carole King and one with co-writer Bill Goss, all for History Press. Karren's Alabama Troubadour book and CD was recently filed with the Alabama Archives. Karren continues to perform with her band and show, The Old Alabama Town Revue, going into its 15th year. This year, 2022, Karren has had two songs released with artists in Canada and Norway. Karren lives in Montgomery in a bungalow that always needs work, with her husband Tim Henderson, and more cats and dogs than she will admit. For more insight, check out Karren's website at: karrenirenepell@wordpress.com